Words of Love

Words of Love

A Healing Journey with the Ten Commandments

EUGENIA ANNE GAMBLE

WESTMINSTER
JOHN KNOX PRESS
LOUISVILLE · KENTUCKY

First edition
Published by Westminster John Knox Press
Louisville, Kentucky

22 23 24 25 26 27 28 29 30 31—10 9 8 7 6 5 4 3 2 1

Unless otherwise indicated, Scripture quotations are from the New Revised Standard Version of the Bible, copyright © 1989 by the Division of Christian Education of the National Council of the Churches of Christ in the U.S.A., and are used by permission.

Book design by Drew Stevens
Cover design by Mary Ann Smith

Library of Congress Cataloging-in-Publication Data

Names: Gamble, Eugenia, 1953- author.
Title: Words of love : a healing journey with the ten commandments / Eugenia Anne Gamble.
Description: First edition. | Louisville, Ky. : Westminster John Knox Press, 2022. | Includes bibliographical references. | Summary: "In the Bible study, Eugenia Anne Gamble dives into each of the Ten Commandments and explores their application as a profound invitation for healing and spiritual transformation for modern-day Christians"—Provided by publisher.
Identifiers: LCCN 2021055874 (print) | LCCN 2021055875 (ebook) | ISBN 9780664267155 (paperback) | ISBN 9781646982349 (ebook)
Subjects: LCSH: Ten commandments. | Spiritual healing. | Spiritual life—Christianity.
Classification: LCC BS1285.52 .G36 2022 (print) | LCC BS1285.52 (ebook) | DDC 241.5/2—dc23/eng/20220111
LC record available at https://lccn.loc.gov/2021055874
LC ebook record available at https://lccn.loc.gov/2021055875

Most Westminster John Knox Press books are available at special quantity discounts when purchased in bulk by corporations, organizations, and special-interest groups. For more information, please e-mail SpecialSales@wjkbooks.com.

To my dear friends and first readers
Mary Newbern-Williams, Martha McDowell,
and Caroline Cohen

CONTENTS

INTRODUCTION

In the summer of 2003, perched alone in a small cabin overlooking the Atlantic Ocean in Nova Scotia, I found myself cross-legged on a scratchy plaid sofa eating macaroni and cheese with cherry tomatoes and watching the evening news. The only station that I could get on the rabbit-eared TV set was an NBC affiliate out of Boston. I was spending a month there on writing leave from my church.

Most days, I rose early and sat on my porch overlooking the sandy beach, sipping coffee and eating Oreo cookies. All morning I read, pondered, took notes, and hoped something profound would occur to me. This particular day, I had given up hope of the profound insight and walked to the little general store in town to buy something for supper, and to look over the dwindling collection of DVDs available for rental. All that was left was a copy of the Mel Gibson flick, *What Women Want*—in German with English subtitles, no less! So, armed with a box of mac and cheese, the tomatoes, a small carton of milk, and *Was Frauen Wollen*, I headed back to my cabin just in time for the nightly news.

I clicked on the TV to see a wild image of the state capital in my home state of Alabama, and what appeared to be a riot. The then-chief justice of the Alabama Supreme Court

1

had defied a federal court order to remove a monument of the Ten Commandments from the capitol rotunda to an art and history room down the hall. On the steps of the capitol, the same steps upon which Dr. Martin Luther King Jr. and the leaders of the civil rights movement had stood and prayed after the long and bloody voting rights march from Selma, throngs of people gathered with signs and shaking fists. Police tried to intervene. At one point, a well-dressed, middle-aged man threw himself on the monument, screaming viciously, "You will not remove my God!"

I was shocked, horrified really. It was, after all, a monument, not God. And wasn't there something written on that very monument about idols anyway? As I sat mesmerized, searching the crowd in the fervent hope that none of my parishioners were there being hauled off in shackles, I began to wonder about that man. It was not so much about his politics and ideology that I wondered. That I recognized. It was his passion that captivated me, the fierceness of it, the utter wildness of his determination to preserve those words on that stone. As I sat there pondering, long after the segment ended, I felt a small question begin to surface in my heart. "Are you, Eugenia, wild for the Word?" That little moment led me to a years-long study of the Ten Commandments and resulted in *Love Carved in Stone: A Fresh Look at the Ten Commandments*, the Horizons Bible study for 2019–2020.

During those years of study and pondering, I led many retreats on the Ten Commandments. Through those retreats and my time traveling the country introducing *Love Carved in Stone*, I continued to learn more and more about the powerful emotions that a deep consideration of the Ten Commandments often engender. I learned that in addition to being a brief outline of basic morality, in addition to being a template for life in community, the Ten Commandments are also a powerful outpouring of God's love for our personal, familial, and societal transformation. It is to that aspect of the Ten Commandments that I turn in this book.

Before we approach the meat of this volume, a few basics will be important for you to master. First of all, the Ten Commandments appear in two different places and forms in the Bible: Exodus 20 and Deuteronomy 5. In most translations, the original text is translated identically into English. In Hebrew, however, there are some differences. Each of those differences offers us a glimpse into a nuance of the text's meaning. I will point those out as we go along.

Second, the text itself does not contain the word "commandment." It appears in our English translations to bracket the text, but it is not in the text itself. The "commandments" are simply called "words" or "utterances." This is very important. It suggests that the Commandments are not simply a list of moral dos and don'ts. They are the *speech* of God. We know from even a cursory reading of Scripture, that God's speech is powerful. It does things. It brings things into being. Think about the creation narratives in Genesis. "And God *said* . . . and it was so." God creates through speech, through words, through utterances.

We can think of the words of God as pure divine energy, creating everything that is. God's speech is like the divine womb in which everything takes shape and out of which everything is born. In this way, when talking about Jesus as the Word of God in flesh we see him as the embodiment of divine life and energy that re-creates that which we ourselves broke or debased.

Throughout this book, I refer to the Commandments as the Words. I do this intentionally because changing our language to reflect the biblical writer's language allows spaces to open up in our sometimes staid interpretations of these familiar words. I also do it because the word "commandment" can make it seem that God is simply telling us what to do and what not to do. It is not that simple. In the Ten Words, God is, in the very speaking of the Words, bringing them into being in our lives and community. We are not left with our own power and determination alone to do the right thing. God combines God's power and essence with our desire to do right and brings an entirely new way of life into being.

Some people resist this, and they can get quite testy about it. To use Word rather than commandment feels to them like it takes away the power of the text, making it a list of suggestions from which we can pick and choose to suit ourselves and our times. Nothing could be further from the truth! To use the biblical language points us to a power far greater than our own. Just as God spoke creation into being, in these Words, God speaks a new community into being. It is a community into which we are invited to join God and each other for the transformation of our own lives and the world.

Third, the early manuscripts of Scripture do not have verse numbers, nor are they divided into chapters. Those conveniences came to us much later. The Ten Words are not numbered, nor are they easily divided. Throughout the centuries, scholars have debated the exact number of the Words and where the divisions fall. Some suggest that what we think of as the first Word is not so much a command as a statement of reality and so combine the first and second Words into one. Some divide the final Word into two. There is no real right or wrong here. For our purposes in this book, I use the traditional Reformed divisions. The substance does not change with the numbering.

Finally, over the years of working with this text in groups and retreat settings, I've found that many of us carry a lot of baggage and pain around the Ten Words. Sometimes that manifests in a feeling of moral guilt at having violated them. Sometimes it is deeper than that. Sometimes it has to do with wounds we have suffered due to brokenness in families or prejudices in society. The Ten Words have a sacred way of bringing those wounds to the surface and at the same time offering healing for them. Such is the power of God's speech. It is to this healing journey that we turn in this book.

CHAPTER 1

⌒⌒⌒

GREETING THE
GOD OF LOVE

Addressing Hurtful Views of God

*Then God spoke all these words: I am the Lord your God, who brought
you out of the land of Egypt, out of the house of slavery; you shall have
no other gods before me.*

Exodus 20:1–3

Several years after my experience in Nova Scotia, I
moved from my home in Birmingham, Alabama, to
the central coast of California. In those intervening years,
I went through a very painful divorce. I felt that failure, as
my dad used to say, like a dead weight sinker. I was fifty
years old and had a string of failed relationships with men in
that half century. I had had a wonderful ministry during all
that time, amazingly enough, due to the grace of God alone.
Still, I was flailing around internally. I knew clearly who I
was as a pastor. I knew my gifts for ministry and many of
my limitations. I was full of confidence in that arena. But at
home, alone, it was different. During the day, when I was
doing my work, I was focused and content. At night, when

the meetings were done, when the to do list was as complete as it was going to get, then, I was restless and frightened. I felt guilty and lonely and like something essential had been lost, amputated, and I could no longer dance.

So, I took a geographic cure, packed up my beautiful loft in downtown Birmingham, said good-bye to a church I adored, and headed west to a little cottage half a block from the Pacific Coast. I worked part-time at a neighboring church and spent the rest of my days working on a book project on the first millennium women martyrs, mystics, and reformers.

After I had been in California a short time, I met the man who is now my husband. Robbie grew up in New York and came to California immediately after returning from his tour of duty in Vietnam. He married and raised a family. He had been divorced for more than ten years when we met, I for only two. He was over it. I was not. But he sure was cute, blue eyes, infectious grin, and the gentlest soul I've ever known. I remember thinking, "Well, what can it hurt to go out to dinner with him?" So, I did, and we began to see each other regularly.

The problem came about a year and a half into our relationship, when he wanted to get married. I did not. I was terrified, certain that I was not good at it and never wanted to go there again. He asked. I said no. Things went on as they had before. About three months later, he asked again. I said no again. Another three months passed. Same thing. Then another three.

One day, we were sitting on a bench by the ocean sharing a sandwich. The sky was bright blue, and the waves crashed powerfully on the rocky coast. Otters played. Herons fished. He asked again. I could feel myself backing up on the bench. He felt it too. Then, he took my face in both of his hands. "Genie," he said. "I am not that other guy. I'm *your guy* and you are safe with me." Now, Robbie is quick to say that I still turned him down that day. But it was a turning point. We were married within the year.

Why do I begin a conversation about the First Word with that story? Because that is how God begins the story, with a powerful declaration of love, of a love that changes everything. Much like a suitor in former times might declare intentions to a dearly loved one, God in the beginning of this new beginning, declares God's self to us. *I am your God.*

Our Divine Love Story

Love, for humans, always has a history. It sometimes hits in a flood of endorphins. Often, though, it hums into our lives like a barely heard vibration of the soul, small experience by small experience. Both of these dynamics can be seen in our love story with God in Scripture.

By the time that Moses makes his trek to the holy mountain to get advice from God about what to do with his unruly, wilderness-weary people, the people of Israel had a centuries-long history of both joy and disappointment in their relationship with God.

Jealousy in the family of Jacob fractured the family and led to Joseph winding up in prison, and then in power in Egypt. Reconciliation between the twelve brothers allowed the family to reunite there and to prosper. But that was long ago. As the people grew in numbers and influence, a new Pharaoh arose who did not remember the old relationships and who saw in the people only what he could get out of them. They became units of productivity and eventually slaves. Life was hard. Scholars disagree about how long this situation lasted. It is clear, in any case, that it lasted for generations.

Moses was born into the harshness of that life of oppression. As is so often the case, oppressors are easily threatened and murder often follows. Pharaoh decided that the sheer numbers of the Hebrew people posed a demographic shift that was a threat to his power. So, he ordered the male children of the Hebrews to be executed. This edict was both diabolical and short-sighted. He was, after all, eliminating his future work force. Still, it is not unheard of in human history for unscrupulous leaders, when frightened, to do cruel things that, in the long run, are not even in their own self-interest.

God is always present and working in circumstances of oppression, even when the evidence is not clear in the moment. In Moses' case, God was at work through the determination, wits, and courage of a remarkable group of women: his mother, sister, two amazing midwives, and a compassionate princess. Moses was spared and grew up in the palace itself as the child of the Egyptian princess.

As a young adult, the streams of Moses' own history came together in another tragedy that changed the trajectory of his life. He saw an Egyptian soldier brutally beating a Hebrew slave. Moses, overcome with rage, killed the soldier. Once he realized what he had done, he buried the soldier in the sand and fled the city for a new life in the wilderness. There he met his wife and went to work for his father-in-law. It was while doing that work that Moses was met with the voice of God calling out to him from a burning bush.

God had work for Moses to do. God wanted him to go back to Egypt, back to the home he had fled in fear, and tell Pharaoh to set the people free. Moses was stunned and reluctant. To do what God desired, he would have to face his past. He would have to go back to the families he had left behind. He would have to risk the consequences of facing his lost loves, his worst failures, and his own murderous impulses. That is the path to transformation for many of us. Still, it is more amazing that he agreed than that he resisted.

In this encounter with the voice of God in the burning bush, Moses made an audacious request. He asked for the gift of God's name. We will talk about the importance of the name in chapter 3, however, at this point, it is important to remember that God said yes to this request and gave Moses the divine name, YHWH (vocalized, when appropriate, as Yahweh). It means *being* itself—"I am who I am" (Exod. 3:14).

Rabbi Rachel Mikva, in *Broken Tablets: Restoring the Ten Commandments and Ourselves*, shares that the early rabbis and scholars of Torah found the word YHWH to be an ecstasy in itself.[1] To hear the word whispered is to be transported out of oneself into the realm of perfect love.

This is how God begins the Ten Words. *I am* (YHWH) yours. Like Robbie taking my face in his hands, the story turns on love. It is God's love that gives us the courage to confront the past, to stand up to the powers, and to move into a different way of life.

Love Is a Journey

Moses, despite his fear and reluctance, did return to Egypt and, by the power of God, he did lead the people out. By the time Moses heads up Mount Sinai for help from God, the people have been in the wilderness for many years. They had, in their opinion, as the old saying goes, traded a headache for an upset stomach. They found fault with nearly everything that God tried to do for them on their journey. Freedom was harder than they thought. So hard that they even began to view slavery in Egypt through rose-colored glasses. At least, they reminisced, we had meat to eat. And weren't the onions in Egypt grand? To ease their hunger and calm their spirits, God sent bread from heaven and quails to eat. Rather than trust God for daily provision, they hoarded what they came to think of as *their* resources and made themselves sick on it.

Not only are the people moaning, griping, and complaining, enemies are finding them even in the wilderness. After a battle with the Amalekites, Moses sends his wife, Zipporah, and their two sons back to her father, Jethro. When they return to the wilderness for a visit, they find Moses completely exhausted from sitting as a judge and arbiter of all of the complaints of the people. Then they come to Sinai.

That is the context for the gift of the Ten Words. Moses is worn out. The people have lost vision. God has so much more for them and us than that. When Moses ascends the mountain, breaks through the clouds and mists, what he finds is more remarkable than he could have dreamed. In the midst of the clouds of power and holiness lies a God who says, "I am yours."

We, too, may know what it is like to find ourselves stuck in places we never intended to stay. We know what it is like to wish for things to go back to the way they were, even while we rewrite that old history to make it seem better than it was. We know what it is like to dismiss or despise the gifts God gives us because they are not the ones we thought we wanted. We know what it is like to feel unsure that God will be there for us each and every day, and so we hoard what resources we are given until they make us sick—literally or spiritually. We know what it is like to want to please God and to also wonder if God is trustworthy at the same time. The wilderness time is not foreign to us.

It is astounding that it is into those times of fear, fatigue, and disillusionment that God moves and says, "I am yours. I belong to you. I declare myself yours." God's self-giving love is the container, a frame within which the Ten Words and all of life are to be understood.

God's love is more, however than a simple frame. It is, perhaps, a *mandorla*. A mandorla is an ancient sacred symbol that gained prominence in Christian art in the Middle Ages. It is that almond shape that is created when two circles intersect. Mandorlas invite us to look deeply through them at those moments when the human and the divine, the mundane and the sacred, intersect. It is the mandorla that holds everything within it together. It provides a boundary, although a mysterious one, and is the context for all that is pictured within it.

Divine Love holds the pieces of life together. Divine Love makes the mundane sacred. Divine Love holds the Ten Words together as one great vision of human and divine life intersecting. Nothing about the Ten Words will be ultimately transformative until we understand that it begins with love, ends with love, and is framed with love. Everything else distorts.

Love Frees

Not only does God declare Godself to us, and in so doing make the new and special relationship a reality, God immediately, upon making that declaration, reminds us of who God really is. "I am the LORD your God, who brought you out of the land of Egypt, out of the house of slavery" (Exod. 20:2).

What must Moses have thought? Did he think that God was simply clarifying which god he was speaking with, lest Moses confuse God with some other divine being that he had heard of, or perhaps wished for, over the years? Or was God, as I believe, reminding Moses of the central characteristic of God for us?

God begins this divine encounter by declaring Godself to us and reminding us that God is the one who sets us free.

God is not a god like Pharaoh, whose entire goal is to be worshiped, served, and enriched. Divine Being, Divine Love, is devoted to setting the beloved free from every bondage that keeps us from the life of promised blessing for which we were created. The freedom Divine Love declares is not just *from* something. It is also *to* something. It is freedom into love, and the resulting life of love, that the Words describe.

In saying that God is the one who brought us out of slavery, God reminds us that what God did for the Hebrew people long ago, God is still doing right here and right now. The organizing intention of Divine Love is always liberation. That liberation mirrors God's own freedom and Jesus' central purpose. In Galatians 5:1, Paul reminds us that it was for freedom that Christ set us free.

How is it that over the centuries so many of us have come to see God differently from that? When presented with God reaching into the muck and mess of human life and offering love and freedom, how is it that we so often choose to focus on God as fierce and disappointed with us instead? Why? Perhaps that, too, has a long history.

Jonathan Edwards, the British colonial pastor and theologian of the Great Awakening in mid-eighteenth century New England, wrote a widely distributed sermon called "Sinners in the Hands of an Angry God." This sermon was filled with images of hell and God's fury with human recalcitrance. It is powerful stuff and a telling glimpse into the theology of God's vengeance as motivation for repentance and change. The image of sinners being dangled by a fierce God over the pits of hell has stuck in our psyches more than we might imagine, leaving us often with a cowering approach to God, if we dare approach at all.

It is not just the fiery rhetoric of the pulpit. Sometimes our own halting reading of Scripture itself has left us wary of the quest to please God. Sometimes it leaves us weary of the quest to even *like* God.

A colleague told me recently of an incident with an acquaintance who contacted her with a poignant question: "How do I read the Bible without being furious with God?" It can be hard work to excavate the God who holds our faces and breathily says, "I'm yours" from the harsh and patriarchal culture through which that revelation comes to us even now.

A few years ago, when I was still pastor in California, Robbie and I went to a wine-tasting event at a local winery. It was my favorite winery, situated on the beautiful sloping hills from which we could watch the fog roll in off the Pacific. This particular evening, I was seated next to a woman who looked familiar to me, although I couldn't place her. As it turned out, she had moved to the Central Coast a few years before from the Midwest, where she had been an active leader in her church. She had visited our church several times and then disappeared. I asked her if she had found a church home. "No," she said. "I liked your church a lot, but I find that I can no longer be associated with what the word Christian has come to mean." Wow. I was speechless. Sometimes, it is those who seek to represent or interpret God who make God either incomprehensible or frightening. People come to think that God hates and refuses to welcome those that the church seems to hate, disregard, or refuse to welcome.

Perhaps even more poignantly, some of us have difficulty imagining ourselves being embraced by Divine Love because of the overemphasis on male parental images of God. It is little wonder that some of us view God through the experiences we have had of maleness and privilege. If those experiences have been largely generous and loving, we tend to see God in the same way. If they have been distant, brutal, or repressive, we see God in that way. If our experiences of male authority have been largely silent, absent, or unreachable, we tend to see God in that way.

My senior year in seminary, I took a practicum class in spiritual direction. Class members volunteered as directees so that we could learn from experience. My directee was a second career man who had worked for twenty years in government. He talked beautifully about his faith in Jesus but when it came to talking about God as Father, he shut down completely. He told me about the hours he had spent as a child locked in a closet by his father, who angrily stood outside the door telling him what a disappointment he was and how he wished he had never been born. For my directee, using male parental language about God was so triggering that he found it hard to even lead the Lord's Prayer.

The rich maternal images of God in Scripture can help us to a degree. Even those, however, are subject to our own experiences. Because all we truly understand in this world we understand in the realm of human experience, it is easy to project our experiences onto God, especially when the God of Scripture chooses to come to us in skin and bone in Jesus.

If our experience of gender identity doesn't fit over-whelming cultural norms, it can be even more complicated to embrace or feel the embrace of a God who is presented to us in stereotypically gendered ways. That is why, in so far as it is practical in English, I avoid gendered pronouns for God at all.

Experiencing Divine Love in Each Other

When I was in college and active in our campus church and ministry, somehow I was put in charge of vacation Bible school. I was an only child who had always lived in an adult world and did not even know how to change a diaper. Nevertheless, I was still young enough, and cocky enough, to feel invincible, so I took on the challenge. I was able to coerce one of my friends, an extraordinarily gifted poet who later became an Episcopal priest, to teach the elementary school group. Everything went beautifully the first day. And the second.

On the third day, my friend Louie came out of his classroom at snack time looking stricken. All the color had drained from his usually ruddy complexion. He looked like a man headed to the gallows. He held in his hand a small stack of papers on which the children had colored pictures. "What happened?" I asked. Quietly he handed me the papers and said, "We were studying Moses going up Mount Sinai and I asked them to draw a picture of what they thought God looked like."

I flipped through the pages. Each page contained a variation of the same image: God with long brown hair, a ruddy complexion, wire-rimmed spectacles and a tie-dyed T-shirt. Each child had drawn Louie. Mercifully, that gentle soul did, in my opinion, point them to a genuine and tender glimpse of the God of Love, but Louie was horrified. It was all I could do to get him to complete the week, so undone was he.

It is indeed humbling to realize how much of what we experience we project onto God. Often, we project our parental pain or comfort onto God. When I was a young child, my father used to come into my room at bedtime for nighttime prayers. He sat at the foot of my bed and taught me how to fold my hands, palms together and fingers pointed toward heaven, with his big hands covering my own. He always asked me three questions to guide our prayer time. "Does anything hurt? Who are you concerned about? Does anyone you know need help?" Then we prayed. As I grew, he taught me the Lord's Prayer and even the Ten Commandments on my fingers. The image of a loving, comforting, guiding father has always been easy for me. Not so for many of us.

Years ago, I heard United Methodist pastor John Sumwalt tell a story about an experience he had one Sunday.

There was a young family in his church at the time. They were regulars. The father, mother, and two small children, sat together near the front of the sanctuary, close to the pulpit. One Sunday, as he preached, John noticed that the father was becoming agitated. At one point, the young man got up and fled down the center aisle of the church, leaving his family embarrassed and confused.

When the man got outside, he was so upset and chagrined that he walked home. He had no idea why he had done what he did. Later that afternoon, he and his wife took a walk to try to sort out what had happened. No luck. She suggested that he might go and speak with the pastor to see if any light could be shed. He agreed and made an appointment for the next day.

When he arrived at the pastor's office, after profuse apologies, the two began to try to understand what happened. John asked the man to tell him what he remembered of the service before he left. He remembered a lot. He remembered the hymns sung and the prayer concerns offered. He remembered the Old Testament lesson but could not recall the Gospel lesson. John picked up his Bible and read that lesson. It was the story of Jesus' baptism. When he got to the end of the passage and read "This is my Son, the Beloved, with whom I am well pleased (Matt. 3:17)," the young man began to shake and burst into tears. "That is always what I longed to hear from my own father," he said through heaving sobs.

For those with painful parental relationships, we can tend to think that God thinks of us as exactly what we think our own parents think of us. More subtly though, we can come to think that God thinks of us as what we think of ourselves. If we have come to a place where we are content with ourselves, appreciate our good qualities, and even recognize the teaching role of our deficits, then we tend to see God as content with us, appreciative of our efforts, and lovingly teaching us to heal through our failures.

However, if we see ourselves as an amalgamation of disappointments and failures, held together by little more than habit and skin, we can find it difficult to cut through that pain to get to God at all. We come to think that God views us through the same filters with which we judge ourselves.

In that case, it can be hard to imagine the love of God for us because we cannot imagine ourselves as loveable or worthy. We may go through the motions of faith, hedging our bets against hell, or hoping for a razzle dazzle miracle that will, in one moment, change our view and heal our hurts, but even that can feel like a sham. If we stay in a place of self-loathing long enough, faith and its practice, and maybe even God, become shallow and transactional at best, shame-filled and numbing at worst.

When God Seems Absent

Sometimes we have difficulty receiving God's love simply because we cannot *feel* God's presence or God seems unresponsive to our prayers or needs. There are times when God's presence is shockingly real. It knocks us to our knees or overwhelms us to tears. It can come in an experience of beauty, an insight, the taste of the sacrament. It can come in the flash of a word of comfort or the understanding eyes of a friend or colleague.

There are many other times when God can seem absent. We knock on heaven's door until our knuckles bleed and receive no answering embrace, just an aching void. We can't understand why God is not helping us. The feeling of abandonment by God can be devastating.

A number of years ago, I had surgery to repair damage to my neck caused by an automobile accident. The surgery was routine. All seemed to go well. I was due to be released from the hospital on a Saturday, but when the surgeon made his rounds to see me, he decided to keep me another night. I just "didn't look right." Later that day, I began to have trouble breathing. I called for help from the nurses' station. They came with a breathing treatment for my asthma. That was not the problem. My breathing became so labored and desperate, that the nursing staff became concerned. Just before I lost consciousness, I heard the nurse say, "Call the code. We are losing her." Then all went to blackness. It was a horrible, horrible feeling of utter fear and aloneness.

I was whisked back into surgery where a bleed was discovered and repaired. Because I couldn't tend to myself for the first two months of recovery, I went home to my parents. That period was a true dark night of the soul. The experience of the code, and the sense of abandonment I had in that moment, consumed me. I was so angry, not that it had happened, but that I hadn't felt God's presence in it. I had had other near-death experiences that had seemed to be infused with light and presence. But this one was truly awful. The more I thought about it, the angrier and more depressed I got. Why wasn't I met by the light? Why didn't an angel come for me? Was it all just a big joke?

My father recognized that I was struggling. One evening he came into my room and sat at the foot of the bed, just like he had all those evenings in my childhood when he was teaching me to pray. He asked me what was wrong. The whole story flooded out of me with all the outrage of a child. I felt about five years old. He listened without comment until I was spent. Then he said, "Well, what makes you think you are better than Jesus?"

This truly infuriated me, and I huffed, "What do you mean?" He said, "As I recall, when Jesus was on the cross he felt abandoned, too. He cried out to his Father, 'Why have you abandoned me?' Maybe that is just part of life."

With those words, something broke open in me. The dark pain seemed to vanish in a breath. I thought how honored I was to have shared that experience with Jesus. I know that sounds pietistic and peculiar, but it happened. I realized then that experiences of absence can be crucial parts of the fullness of human life. For those of us who are Christians, we believe that God chose to come to us in flesh and experienced all things with us, not only to save us from sin and death, but to show us the fullness of life. When I felt that God had abandoned me at the point of death, I was undone. When I realized that God in Christ had had the same experience, that it was just part of human life itself, I was reborn. Love and intimacy can come in many ways, even in what feels like absence.

To submit to the inner transformation of the Words requires some version of the fundamental struggle that Jesus underwent in Gethsemane. With the cross looming, he asked to be spared. In his anguish he finally came to a moment when he said to God, "nevertheless," not my will but yours be done. Even if Divine Love takes us to the garden of betrayal, to the time of dashed expectations, to the cross of abandonment, it is always on the way to new life. If we want to enter into a healing journey with the Words, then we will have to overcome our habitual resistance to transformation's ways with our own "nevertheless." Until then the Words remain either chains to resent, quaint admonitions to ignore, or else weapons with which to bludgeon others to make ourselves feel righteous.

Sometimes we struggle with Divine Love because, if we can conceptualize love at all in our wounded state, it is conditional at best. The problem with that view is that there is no such thing as conditional love. Conditions are just blocks that we put up to giving and receiving love. They may sometimes be necessary, for example, to protect ourselves from toxic relationships and danger, but they are still blocks. God does not block.

The beginning of the Ten Words tells us that God's love is not conditional. Our lives and choices can certainly throw up blocks to our living in the vastness of God's freeing love, but that is us and not God. Only as we learn to love and be loved can we approach anything like freedom.

Conclusion

When we release and sink into the First Word, the change in us is profound and the other Words naturally flow. They become an expression of who we truly are because of who God truly is. This does not mean that we will never fail, that we will never forget who and whose we are. It just means that Divine Love and freedom daily become a more settled truth in us and less a matter up entirely to our wills. When we return the embrace, it becomes an easier and shorter trip to come home.

The Ten Words begin with profound, nearly unimaginable, love and self-giving on God's part. They begin with a call to remember that God longs for nothing more than to set us free from any bondage or pain. In order for that to happen, sometimes we must heal our relationship with God and with ourselves. Then we can turn to and deal with those things that we have looked to for love and help that can never actually deliver. That is the work of the Second Word.

Spiritual Practice: Addressing Hurtful Views of God

In the Gospel of Mark, Jesus' first instruction to the people is the Greek word *metanoete*, "repent." We often think that it is a synonym for remorse. We think it means to feel sorry for a moral failing or an immoral action. To repent, for us, is to say, "I'm sorry." With this understanding it is perfectly possible to be sorry for something and to change nothing.

The word that Jesus uses is much bigger than that. *Metanoete* means to have a fundamental change of mind, world view, or way of processing things. It means to change and go another way.

Repentance, primal change, is always deliberate. We choose, by the grace of God, to think different thoughts. If we find ourselves thinking, "I'm old, fat, and unlovable," then we can choose to stop in the midst of that thought and replace it with another thought such as "I'm wise, creative, and beloved of God." Even if the new thought seems ridiculous or doesn't "feel" true, we can do it anyway. It is especially effective to speak the new thought out loud. As we do that, just as God did in creation and in the Ten Words, we begin to create a new reality.

Obviously, saying something is so does not make it automatically a reality if it defies the laws of physics. If I am 66 years old, I can't say out loud that I am 22 and have my physical body obey. What I can say is "I am strong, resilient, and powerful." Before I know it, my choices and my circumstances will begin to align with that truth. We change ourselves and we change the world with how we choose to think about it.

The easiest and most profound way to start this *metanoeite* practice is to reframe your thoughts with gratitude. For example, if you are struggling to overcome an unhealthy habit, you might begin by noticing all of the healthy habits you do have. If you can't seem to shake a pervading sadness or if grief and loss are consuming you, try to make a list each day of five blessings. Some days we can just write "I made it through" five times.

Try to practice awakening to the small graces with which each day is filled, a warm cup of tea, a nuzzle from a beloved pet, a full moon, and a sky full of stars. Just choosing to notice those blessings gives you a measure of power and pushes, for a split second, other more painful thoughts to the periphery. We will return to gratitude practice again and again as we make our healing journey with the Ten Words.

Today, in whatever circumstance or challenge you face, choose to repeat to yourself: *God loves me and sets me free.* With that repetition, over time, you will find that internal shifts begin to happen and healing will take place.

Questions for Personal and Group Reflection

1. At some point in life, did you learn that love was outside of you, somehow owned or controlled by others and meted out by the other's pleasure or displeasure? Reflect for a moment on how that happened.

2. Was the image of God's fierce anger used to control you? Was the fear of hell used to scare you into domesticity, scare you into faith and commitment? If so, what was the result?

3. Why do you think this pain around love persists for you?

4. What do you need in order to see Divine Love as the mandorla around the Ten Words, and around your own life?

5. From what do you need to be freed? From whose voice do you need to be set free?

CHAPTER 2

～～

LOOKING FOR A GOD
THAT SPARKLES

Addressing Destructive Allegiances

*[Y]ou shall have no other gods before me. You shall not make for
yourself an idol, whether in the form of anything that is in heaven
above, or that is on the earth beneath, or that is in the water under
the earth. You shall not bow down to them or worship them; for I the
LORD your God am a jealous God, punishing children for the iniquity of parents, to the third and fourth generation of those who reject
me, but showing steadfast love to the thousandth generation of those
who love me and keep my commandments.*

Exodus 20:3–6

In the summer of 2004, I had the opportunity to take a sabbatical from my parish ministry to spend three months as
a guest of the Evangelical Reformed Church of the Canton
of Zürich in Switzerland. During that time, I visited a number of old churches. Many of them were pre-Reformation
churches that had become Reformed in the sixteenth century. In several of those churches, artisans were carefully
trying to remove the whitewash in the sanctuaries that had

been applied by the Reformers to cover the religious art on the walls. In their zeal, they took the Second Word literally. No images. They believed that God was so vast as to be impossible to represent. Therefore, any attempted representation was, by definition, a distortion. Images limited God and were therefore a stumbling block to piety.

So, is God asking us to knock out the stained glass in our churches? To take a hammer to the Pietá? To cover the Sistine Chapel with a couple of coats of Benjamin Moore? For that matter, is God asking me to remove the little statue of the risen Christ that is sitting on my desk right now? Or my beloved icon of the Virgin and Child? What is really the threat from which God is trying to protect us here?

In the Hebrew Scriptures, idols are generally physical representations of a deity or power that people choose to worship. The golden calf is an example of this. Such idols are considered *hebel*, that is, worthless or insubstantial. They are not so much essentially evil as essentially useless. Another group of words describing idols, or images, comes from the word for dung pellets, hence, useless refuse. All of that tells us that idols or images have no power at all. They can never do for us what we want them to do, and they can become toxic. Images may be lovely, our idols may sparkle like a golden calf. They may help us feel better or righteous in our serving them, but they make poor gods.

Idolatry comes in many forms. Before we explore further, it may be helpful to understand some of the harsh-sounding words in these verses. A jealous God? A punishing God? A God of steadfast love? Which is it? What is going on here?

God's Zeal

The word we translate into English from the Hebrew as "jealous" means to be filled with righteous zeal or passion.

It is used to speak of someone who stakes a claim on another to the exclusion of all other claimants. So, rather than depicting God as an insecure lover who lashes out when feeling threatened, this word tells us that God is zealously passionate for our well-being. That passion issues in God's exclusive claim on our hearts and loyalty. God recognizes that no secondary allegiance we might have can ever do for us what only God can do. God has declared Godself to be our One and knows that unless God is also our Only, our love story will go awry.

Actually, God has seen this in us before. In the stories of our beginnings in Genesis, we find that we are created for a life of abundance, peace, love, and intimacy with God in the garden of Eden. All of our needs are lavishly met. We are surrounded by beauty and everything is sustainable. That is, until we decide that we want more, that the fruit of the out-of-bounds tree is more alluring than all the others. It looks delicious. What could it really hurt? Besides, we are told that this dazzling fruit has the added bonus that, once we have eaten it, we will cross the boundary of our created nature and be like God. Look where that got us.

In Hebrew, the phrase "punishing children for the iniquity of parents" reads "visiting the iniquity of fathers on the children." The word "iniquity" usually refers to something that is faulty, mischievous, or punishing. Most often it is collective, referring to groups or peoples. In those instances, it suggests the painful consequences of the aggregate of crooked behavior that is the result of the sum of past sin. It is also used to refer to individual choices and the aggregate consequences of them.

Sin and consequences are more intimately related in the Old Testament than we sometimes think today. You cannot have one without the other. The idea of someone getting away with something, not getting caught and paying a price, is unimaginable. In the Hebrew mind that would be a sin itself, an affront to God's holiness and justice.

In the thinking of our ancestors, there was no such thing as a secondary cause. Anything that happened, God did it, or actively made room for it. So there was no frame of reference for the idea of an unintended or unjust consequence. That is the theological position with which the book of Job struggles.

So what does this phrase mean for us? It means that sin leaks. The accumulation of a lifetime's (or a community's) moral failure has generational consequences. God is passionately zealous for our well-being and tells us that when we fail to follow the God of Love and Freedom and choose ineffective substitutes instead, we will pay a price that will affect others long after we are gone. To be free to choose love is to be free to experience the consequences of loving poorly or serving the wrong things.

There is hope and kindness in these verses, too. Even when consequences come, they are limited. Generational pain does not go on ad infinitum. God puts a boundary to even the pain we continually choose. Iniquity continues to the fourth generation, but blessing for righteousness goes on to the thousandth.

In these harsh-sounding verses, we see that God recognizes that we sometimes hate and turn from what is good for us, and that turning can cause damage for generations when we do. God reminds us that even then, grace is bigger than our pain. It is more lasting.

In describing God's love for us, God uses a foundational word in the theology of covenant. The word in Hebrew is *hesed*. We translate it as steadfast love or loyalty. I like to translate it as God's "unshake-off-able-ness." God's love can never be shaken off, no matter how many wrong turns we take. Sin may leak, but God's love always floods.

It is easy for us, who have been molded into a dualistic view of reward or punishment, to get sidetracked by this punitive language. In the Bible, though, even consequences have a saving purpose. In the book of Ezekiel (16:1–63), the prophet uses the word "restore" to talk about God's punishment. In that sense, punishment is not a function of wrath, but of love. It can only consist of that which restores, never that which utterly destroys. The cross and the empty tomb model that truth.

Choosing and Rejecting

Perhaps it will help us at this point to pause here and think a bit about the nature of rejecting, or disobedience itself, as used in the Second Word. In Exodus 20:5, the word we translate as "reject" literally means "to hate." Dire consequences come when we choose hate over love. When we hate, we, by definition, reject. All hate is dangerous because the line between what we hate and reject and who we hate and reject is thin and easily crossed. To hate or reject God's ways is especially dangerous.

The word "keep" in this passage means to put a hedge around something to protect it. It means to guard, to preserve, to keep safe, to attend to, to revere, to pay careful attention to.

Obedience, or keeping, is not simply about moral perfection. Keeping is about paying attention, guarding the values of God in life and community. It is not about never making a mistake. God's deepest will is that we take God seriously. The Trappist monk and mystic Thomas Merton put it this way:

The will of God is not a "fate" to which we must submit, but a creative act in our life that produces something absolutely new, something hitherto unforeseen by the laws and established patterns. Our cooperation consists not solely in conforming to external laws, but in opening our wills to this mutually creative act.[1]

God stays true to Godself no matter what we do. God is not a puppet whose strings we pull by our behavior. Otherwise, we would own or control God. That is ridiculous. Our lives and choices affect God, without a doubt. They just do not control God. God will love us unilaterally if it comes to that. God always awaits us at the point of our failure, sewing us new clothes like God did for Adam and Eve after their fall.

The Words are not hoops to jump through in order to please God or be accepted as God's child. They are a sacred reference point. In them, we begin to see who we really are. When we violate, or fail to keep the Words, it is because we are still looking outside of the God of Love for something or someone to define us, or to make us feel better about the discomfort of our inner state of restlessness and homesickness. Those things or people to which we turn can become our idols. We wind up "keeping" the wrong things and "hating" the right One. When we do this for long, our lives become full of contradictions and leave us lonely, insecure and dangerous.

The Challenges to Keeping

It is sometimes difficult for us to keep or obey the Words because we are locked in a system of thought that is motivated mainly by reward or punishment meted out to us from either the pleasure or the disappointment of God rather than seeing our lives as part of an eternal flow of love and justice. In that system, we have all the control. We come to think that our will, or lack thereof, is more powerful than any flow of God. We forget the love story into which we have been drawn and we forget that the Ten Words are essentially a love letter that celebrates the life we live within God's divine embrace.

Thinking solely of right versus wrong, perfect or punished, is a recipe for resentment. Immersed in that system, we come to think of obedience as being externally required of us, *or else*. Fear of punishment may motivate behavior but, in my experience, it rarely leads to lasting transformation and healing.

The reward/punishment system can lead to an opposite problem as well. When, by sheer dint of will, we wrangle our behavior into line long enough, we can begin to think that God owes us a present, or an answered prayer, or just some kind of a break. This is sneaky.

Shortly after I moved to California, my beloved keeshond, Keesie, died. She had been my constant companion during the difficult days of my divorce and its aftermath. When I wiped tears, she licked them from my fingers. Keesie did not just die. She was seventeen, very old for that breed, and her arthritic pain had gotten so bad that it couldn't be managed. She could hardly stand. The day I took her to the vet, her eyes asked me to let go. It was awful. For years I had prayed for two special blessings from God: that I would never divorce and that I would never have to put a pet to sleep. I was 0 for 2.

That night when I came home to my empty house, I was undone. I was furious with God. Had I not given my life to God's church? Sure, I hadn't been perfect. But still. As I fumbled with my keys, thinking of the soft fur and kind heart of my pet, I remember shouting out to God, "Couldn't you have at least spared me that? You are not the God I wanted!"

In times like that, when what we really want is just to stop hurting, it is helpful to remember that life with God is never intended to be a quid pro quo. It is an outpouring of love that may not look like we expect it to at all. This can be especially difficult to see when we have made what we want, or think we deserve, into an idol itself. That is always a function of our own pain to one degree or another. As the old spiritual saying goes, "Most people do not see things as they really are. We see things as *we* really are."[2] What we need to remember is that idols always lie.

The Invitation of the Second Word

The Second Word invites us to remember where our real source of love and power lies and to stop wasting time on lesser powers that are ineffective at best, and "dung pellets" at worst.

The problem is that we do not always recognize our idols as such. Often, we think they are necessary or inescapable. Sometimes we call them gifts or rights. Sometimes they are so deeply entrenched in our psyches that we can't tell their voices from God's.

Many of the things we make into idols are deeply cherished, like our families, our churches, or our political ideologies. Most are not evil in and of themselves. There is nothing intrinsically evil about a family member, a preference, a political party, or religious art on a church wall. Those things are just useless as gods. When we serve them as if they were God, we take what can be a gift and turn it into a tyrant that can stop our ability to grow and make putting God first difficult.

Sometimes our idols are not as much useless things as misused things. Relationships are a good example of this. Our relationships are crucial to our lives. We love and need to pay attention to them. A lot of attention. When, however, they begin to dictate to us values or behaviors that are contrary to God's values, when we do not feel secure in them, or when we allow the ones we love to call all the shots in our lives to the point we are depleted, then we are serving them as masters. Sadly, that serves not only God poorly, but the ones we love poorly as well.

When we cannot identify and release ourselves from the hold the idols we serve have over us, we not only forget who and whose we are, but in our drive to fill the holes in our lives that result from this amnesia, we use the ones we love as a fix for our hurts or fears. They become objects to be used and, instead of freeing and joyous, our love becomes needy and self-centered. Idols can never do for us what we think they can.

We can idolize people or our inner imagining of who they are or should be or do. It is common to idolize the idealized family or our role in it. You don't have to scratch the surface of church life to hear someone say, when making an excuse for not participating in this or that, "Family comes first." Well, no. God comes first. Of course, whatever church activity that led to the sheepish excuse is no more God than the child's soccer game or birthday party. The issue is what or who rules us. Is it Divine Love or is it something or someone else?

The capacity to discern the useless (or the misused) from the divine lies within each of us. Howard Thurman, in his baccalaureate address to Spelman College in May 1980, put it this way:

There is something in every one of you that wants and listens for the sound of the genuine in yourself. It is the only true guide you will ever have. And if you cannot hear it, you will all of your life spend your days on the ends of strings that somebody else pulls.[3]

God does not want us as frustrated and confused puppets. God wants us centered and filled with God's power and grace. It is in that state that Divine Love transforms us, bit by bit, and we become people capable of loving others in kind.

Idols Can Be Anything

In the spring before I retired, I again had spinal surgery. It was successful but had unintended consequences that required my retirement. During the months that I was bedridden, I was in both physical and emotional pain. It was Lent and I was not in my church. I was totally bereft. Early in Lent, one of my parishioners gave me a beautiful book of paintings and sculptures of the face of Jesus from all over the world. I loved it. I lay in bed and just held it and cried. Was that a violation of the Second Word?

I guess it depends. Great religious art can be used by God to console and inspire. Artists can be used by God to create and in so doing elevate the spirit. The problem comes when we confuse the creation with the Creator and choose to serve the one above the other. Did that lovely book substitute for God for me? Or did it serve as an icon or touchstone to keep me connected to God and the love of my church? Some minutes it was one. Some minutes it was the other.

Our idols can be anything. They can be habits, compulsions, addictions, ways of doing things, timelines, goals, our self-image, or our inner critic. We can make idols of our own hurts, wounds, fears, or the distorted stories we tell over and over again about ourselves.

Perhaps the stories we tell ourselves about ourselves, and the ways we serve those stories, are the most potent idols of all. Growing up as a chronically ill child, I came to fear that I was defective. I couldn't run like the other kids. I missed a lot of school. I believed that there was always something the other children could do that I could not or that they had learned that I had not.

My way of compensating for that was to develop the story line of being exceptional. I never felt that I had to be perfect, just that I had to somehow shine a little brighter than most. I didn't have to get 100 percent on every test. I just had to be in the top three that got 98 percent. That was a potent and sometimes devastating idol to worship. It still is.

My first call in ministry was to work for my denominational headquarters in the area of leadership development for women. In that capacity, I spent much of my time traveling and leading workshops and retreats. I accepted every invitation; after all, I had to be exceptional. One summer I scheduled eight back-to-back events with only a day or two at home to wash my clothes. For each event, I prepared a customized presentation.

By the time I reached the last event, I was emotionally, physically, and spiritually spent. When I got off the airplane and met the smiling retreat team with their welcome signs and balloons, I could not remember why I was there or what I had agreed to do.

That evening the retreat team met to go over details with each leader. Did we have what we needed in our rooms? Did we have our class lists? By this time, I had a screaming headache and all I wanted in the world was to go to my room, take a couple of Tylenol, and get some sleep.

At the end of the meeting, the retreat leader asked us all to stand in a circle, hold hands and pray. As she and others prayed, the best I could do was pray, "Dear God, please let these people stop praying so I can go to my room!" At one point, I remember someone praying, "Dear God, please let each person here know that what he or she brings is enough." That shot to my heart. I began to weep. I could not remember ever feeling that anything I did or was, was enough. Taking deeply held idols such as that from their pedestals can be the work of a lifetime, but it is the essential work of a lifetime.

We may not recognize our most deeply entrenched idols until a tipping point is reached and our lives become unmanageable due to their demands and we wind up, in one way or another, sobbing in front of a room full of strangers who paid good money to learn from us. Or, worse by far, when in our exhaustion from serving the wrong things, our love turns cold. When we forget who we belong to and give ourselves away to whatever seems to patch a hole or sparkle in the moment, our idols will insert and assert themselves with pain, fear, stress, anxiety, or, horrifyingly, with self-congratulation.

The wiliest idols we serve are so often born of the wounds or fears that we carry. They are ways of trying to heal wounds that we have not allowed, or simply not known how to allow, God to make whole. Wholeness is God's intent for us. It is what the word we translate as salvation means in the Bible. Salvation is not only for the next life. It is God's vision and intention for us now. Idols make that wholeness illusive.

The idols to which we cling most tenaciously inevitably do the exact opposite of what we intend. Think, for example, about my idol of being exceptional. The fear that fed it was of being defective and therefore not a real part of the group. If one has to be exceptional to not feel defective, then by definition, one is separated from the group. That is completely self-defeating. Here again, we see the Bible's wisdom. An idol is useless to get what we really need or want.

Subconsciously, we can also make idols out of coping or survival skills that we needed at one time, but that no longer serve our lives or spiritual growth. For example, if you learned as a child that your environment at home was unsafe or precarious, perhaps you developed the habit of being scrupulously organized and tidy. Now that you are in a more stable and happier environment, you find that you create havoc and judgment in your relationships when your spouse doesn't wipe her feet or hang up his coat. Having things in order gave you a measure of control and security in a chaotic childhood. Being overly insistent upon it now can create more chaos than security in your new family life. Identifying those old coping mechanisms that have become habits that do not serve the present moment takes work. It is not as easy as whitewashing away a picture on the wall.

Habits and compulsions can become addictions that rule our lives and numb us to our true identity as God's beloveds. In serving them, we think we are saving ourselves, but we are really killing ourselves. We may manage our emotions for a moment, but we damage our true selves in the long run. Sometimes we no longer recognize what is genuinely and truly us. We only relate to our habits, our chronic thought patterns, or the parts of ourselves that we can stand to see. We can do this to the point that both the idol we create and the wound it is intended to salve become invisible to us. When we do this for long enough, then our precious self, that is created to be loved by God, and to love God in return, can become buried deeply indeed.

We can also make idols of the things we most despise. We can become obsessed with a politician we loathe, or a sports team whose colors even make us queasy. Or the person who got the promotion we thought we were due. Or a church or denomination or practice that we reject. We can become so consumed with this sense of wrongness or unfairness that the one we despise takes up more space in our hearts and minds than that which we actually support or the God who loves us all and abhors our divisions. One has to look no farther than political attack ads to see it. Rarely is what we stand for as prominent as who and what we despise. Unfortunately, we also see the short-term effectiveness of that idolatry. This is one of the hard things about idols: at first, they seem to work. It is only later that we realize that we ourselves have become what we most deplore.

Idols Everywhere!

Idols can be created to meet a whole host of unexamined needs, fears, habits, or power struggles. An example of an idol that arose from a not-so-subtle church power struggle always makes me smile. I was pastor of a smallish city church that was in the process of rebuilding from a series of losses resulting from a changing neighborhood and the lessening priority of church in the community. I was a part of a group of pastors in similar churches throughout the city.

One day, as we sat down for our regular meeting, one of our colleagues came into the room late and full of life. We had never seen him so buoyant. He looked ten years younger. A new family had joined his church the week before! It had been some time since anyone new had come to his church. There was a feeling of lightness all around. It was May and the positive energy kept up the whole summer.

In September, our first week of meeting after all of our churches had resumed their fall activities, our friend came in totally crestfallen. Something was very wrong. We waited for him to tell us. His church had Wednesday night potluck fellowship suppers during the school year. They had resumed the night before. Each family brought a dish to share and took it into the kitchen and gave it to the person in charge. It was her job to keep hot things hot and cold things cold, and to replace and replenish the dishes on the long serving table as needed.

It was the new couple's first pot-luck, and they brought the wife's specialty for the buffet: a Jell-O salad. It was full of fruit, nuts, and pretzels and was covered with Cool Whip and maraschino cherries. Her husband declared it was world famous and the best food ever invented.

All went according to plan until everybody lined up to be served and the husband noticed that the Jell-O salad was not on the serving table. His wife went into the kitchen to retrieve it just in time to see the person in charge scraping the salad down the garbage disposal.

"What are you doing?" the new member asked.

"Honey," the other woman replied. "You are new here, and you will learn. But we don't use Cool Whip in this church. It is tacky."

I kid you not. We can make idols of anything, even what type of whipped topping we can use. Those idols have the power not only to hurt us, but hurt others, too. That church was roiled by this event and, to my knowledge, never really recovered. Enslavement to our habits, traditions, or processes can have lasting consequences.

In churches, we can make idols of the flowers, the music, the time of worship, the paint colors, the norm for dress, the priority of children and youth. If we do this, then we can find ourselves grinding our teeth in worship when we don't know a hymn, cringing at the new rug in the narthex, or having our peace wrecked by clashing floral arrangements. What was intended to elevate, glorify, and uplift no longer points to God but only brings to the surface our egos' unmet needs. The thing that was so important to us only serves to distract us from that which could actually heal us.

During the isolation of the COVID-19 pandemic, many church members painfully faced the idols we have about what church "should" be like. We bucked and kicked about worshiping online. We could not imagine sharing

Communion around a computer screen until we were forced to do it, and we found that God is not corralled in our traditions or preferences. Jesus can still walk through locked doors or even unstable internet connections.

We can make idols of deeply held values, such as personal freedom—good things that we may give a wrong priority. During the early months of the pandemic, the governor of Alabama closed our beaches to try to flatten the infection curve. The response was pretty predictable. People in Gulf-front properties kicked up a stink. "I can't even walk my dog on my own property! We've become a police state! It's a hoax. I refuse to live in fear and wear a mask." Of course, inconvenience is not the same thing as oppression. What these responses made me ponder was what really rules us and how tenaciously we cling to our idols even when the results cause harm.

While many of the things that we make into idols are neutral until they take a disproportionate place in our lives, other things are intrinsically evil to start with. White supremacy is one example. If you are white in the United States, you live in the stew of it even if you don't feel hatred or superiority, and are appalled at the extremists. The fact that whiteness is the unquestioned "default" is revealed in TV, advertising, de facto segregation in neighborhoods, inequities in education, opportunity, available healthcare, language, voting restrictions, and policing. It is everywhere, even in our casual speech. If we are white, we never speak of a friend as our "white" friend but often specify the race of our non-white friends. This reinforces whiteness as the norm and anything else as the deviation.

My point here is not to address that particular idol directly. My point is to show that cultures and power structures themselves are not immune from creating idols and serving them, with far-reaching consequences. Cultures can create, and serve to the death, wrong things in order to provide a sense of identity, esteem, power, control, or simply to staunch fear.

Idols are all about meeting needs that we think are essential and that we think God either can't or won't meet. God wants us to know that it is God alone, in a myriad of ways and surprising forms, who sustains, heals, directs, restores, loves, and gives us identity and purpose. When we use lesser things to try to meet deeper needs, they inevitably become enslavements, oppressors that have the capacity to fragment our lives and selves and leave us in pieces.

Given, then, that idols can be just about anything, how do we know if we are treating something idolatrously? Asking the following questions may help.

1. Does the thing you are considering, when you let it call the shots in your life, make you more genuinely loving, or more needy, stressed, ashamed, resentful, or entitled? If the latter, it may be an idol in your life.
2. Is the thing worthy of your allegiance? Does it actually sustainably do what you hoped it would do? If not, but it still rules too much of your life, it may be an idol.
3. Does the thing connect you not only to what is most deeply true about God, but also to what is most deeply true about you at your core? Do you have to be somebody inauthentic to serve it? If the latter, it may be an idol.
4. Does it create space for divine relationship or substitute for it? If it crowds out God, that is a good indication it has become an idol.
5. Does it create fear or anxiety in you? Idols are insatiable because they can't do what we are trying to get them to do. This often causes fear and anxiety.

In the Words, our freeing God invites us to choose life, love, and healing and to refuse anything that distorts love, blurs God's image or our truest selves. To banish the idols in our lives is to commit to a lifelong journey of discovery and healing. Each layer of fear-fueled substitutes that we uncover will enable us to uncover the fear that lies behind the idol, the wound we thought it would heal, and the self we left behind to follow it. When we leave the idols behind, what is left is the love story.

Conclusion

Addressing and releasing our idols is not as easy as making a determination of the will that, at least today, we will not obsess about our work or the decorations for our child's birthday party. Desecrating idols is not fundamentally about controlling yourself. Rather it is about meeting yourself in the embrace of Divine Love and returning that embrace. From that place of shared love, new and more authentic choices will emerge, and you can set your foot to a new path.

I have found that there is rarely long-term success in desecrating idols by violent means. If we attack them as monsters, we will not easily hear their messages, or more importantly, the message that God sings behind them. When we gently stop to examine what we have substituted for the love story for which we were born, all we will find behind those substitutes is a love greater than we knew.

In the Second Word, God invites us to look behind the excuses, behind the subtle "pharaoh voices" of our bondage that tell us that our only hope is to turn back to slavery. This Word asks us to turn and embrace the One who not only knows, but created, all of who we are and loves us for all eternity. When we do that, our fears and insecurities become unnecessary. Our destructive ways can be over-come just as the waters covered the advancing army sent by Pharaoh to return the people of Israel to bondage. As God becomes our One and Only, that transformative love begins to flow through us and change both our relation-ships and our communities.

Spiritual Practice: Breath Prayer

Breath prayer is a practice especially well-suited to address idols and enslavements. It is an ancient form of contem-plative prayer in which we quiet our minds, stop chasing our thoughts, and follow our breath into a place of open-ness and Divine Presence. To do this practice, find a com-fortable place where you will not be interrupted. You may want to light a small candle or bring a centering object like a cross or an icon or a seashell to set the space apart as holy.

In breath prayer, we choose a word to repeat as a touch-stone for the prayer. It can be anything you choose. For our purposes, I suggest you use the prayer "I Am Yours." As you take a deep breath in, silently say "I Am." This is both a statement of your being and God's Divine name (YHWH). On the out breath say, "Yours." As you con-tinue in prayer, you may find that you experience a deep sense of Presence that goes beyond any words. You can then drop the verbal prayer and just breathe in and out in the restoring presence of Divine Love. You may not expe-rience that at all. That does not mean that your prayer was ineffective or that you did it wrong. You got and gave what was needed. Try this prayer for ten minutes to start.

Do not be concerned if you lose your concentration or your to do list comes flooding into your mind. You may find old hurts surface or even fantasies of different outcomes to situations. Don't try to wrestle them to the ground. They are a part of you too and not unknown to God. Just let them drift through without giving them any energy. You might imagine those thoughts as bubbles floating on the air. They will go their own way and burst when no longer needed. Just return to the phrase "I Am Yours." It is enough. You are enough. God is enough.

Questions for Personal and Group Reflection

1. How do you see idols at work these days?
2. Do you notice anything in your own life that you cling to unhelpfully? What things tend to guide your moods?
3. How do you see "fear" as an idol? How do we serve that fear?
4. What things do you sometimes put before God in your life?
5. What habits or traditions would be most difficult for you to relinquish? How do you serve them? Have you experienced any negative consequences for that?

CHAPTER 3

∞∞∞

LANGUAGE THAT LIFTS

Addressing the Trivializing of God

You shall not make wrongful use of the name of the Lord *your God,*
for the Lord *will not acquit anyone who misuses his name.*

—Exodus 20:7

R ecently I saw a short video posted online. It featured a family presenting their three- or four-year-old child with a puppy. The child was ecstatic. She picked up the puppy from the box and, literally, ran around the living room for several minutes screaming "Oh my God! Oh my God! Oh my God!" The parents were laughing as they filmed her joy. It was a moment of pure bliss and I smiled too. For a minute. Then, unbidden, something came up from my soul, a thought, "The thing I miss most these days is reverence."

Where did that come from? After all, is using God's name in this kind of innocent joy really a wrongful use? The Third Word will help us decide.

What is so important about how we speak of God? What is so important that God says in this Word that all of

God's love and devotion toward us will not protect us from the consequences of defying it?

In the introduction, I suggested that the Words are God's powerful speech. It is through speech that God creates, shapes, guides, and saves. It is no accident that Jesus is called the *Logos* (Word) of God in John's Gospel. Speech does things and God's speech always, without exception, does creative and loving things.

Created in the image of God, marred though we may be, human speech is powerful as well. In the Hebrew Scriptures, our ancestors understood the power of speech for good and ill. In either case, speech creates a reality that is difficult to turn around. We see this in the story of Jacob and his mother Rebekah colluding to trick Isaac, into giving him the blessing set aside for the firstborn brother, Esau. Once spoken, the words have power. They cannot simply be reversed by uttering other words.

Words stick, and it seems that hurtful ones stick more easily than loving ones. Words of criticism shape relationships, as do words that manipulate or trivialize the ones to whom the words are spoken. Apparently this is even true in nature. Studies by Japanese researcher Masaru Emoto have shown that water crystals form differently when spoken to.[1] When cursed, they become misshapen and deformed. When blessed, they are symmetrical, strikingly beautiful, and unique. Destructive or denigrating speech not only hurts the object but also slowly erodes the soul of the one who speaks it, allowing falsehood to appear true, and making the heart grow cold.

Interpreting this Word broadly, many ancient rabbis taught about the moral imperative to use words that lift as opposed to words that wound. Hurtful words, called the *lashon ha-ra*, were so much to be avoided that the faithful were urged not even to curse a deaf person. Even if the one you curse can't hear you, it is a basic misuse of the gift of speech itself, is therefore immoral, and will damage the person doing the cursing. The gift of human speech is given to connect, bless, glorify, and uplift. It is never to destroy, denigrate, trivialize, or ridicule. Not other people. And not God.

The Power of Names

The concept of naming in Scripture is more than a designation so that we can tell each other apart. Naming is, by itself, an act of intimacy and connection. Four years ago, when our first granddaughter was born, our son and daughter-in-law took their time in naming her. I was beside myself waiting for that name. I could lift her little self up to God for blessing and protection unnamed, but when they called to tell us that her name was Penelope Rose, everything changed. No longer was she just a little bundle of beauty, she somehow newly belonged to us, newly related to us. Her name touched me in a way that baby girl Phillips did not.

For our biblical ancestors, naming initiated a relationship. It shaped the namer as well as the one named. When Adam is given the gift to name the animals, that comes with the responsibility to care for those named. (That is what is meant by dominion in that story. Dominion is not about controlling and using. It is about caring for and ensuring the good of the other.) One of the Greek words most often used in the New Testament for love, *agape*, has that same quality. It is not so much a feeling as an ethic. To do *agape* is to unconditionally seek the good of the other. Naming is powerful, and just like loving, it involves commitment.

In the Bible, names are chosen quite deliberately to describe character or to instill important qualities. Names were often changed, or new names given, after decisive moments that changed the direction of a person's life or marked a real change in character. After answering God's unexpected call, Abram and Sarai become Abraham and Sarah. When the long-awaited child of promise arrives, he is named Isaac, which means laughter, joy. When Jacob, which means usurper, wrestles all night long with God, his name is changed to Israel, which means "he who strives with God." A name carries the person's essential qualities. Those qualities are tied to the relationship with the named one.

Last summer, a high school friend was in town and we met for breakfast at the local Waffle House. We ate and chatted about this and that and nothing. At one point, the subject of my father came up. I don't recall how. Between spoonfuls of scrambled eggs, my friend casually said, "Your father was a hero." I was taken aback. To me, he was just "Daddy" with all the kindness and devotion that name carries for me. But to my friend, he was the attorney and later judge who tried some of the most famous civil rights cases in our state. Names occur in relationship and in context.

To make a name for oneself was about reputation in the Bible. It was also about longevity. A name lives on, as a reputation lives on. The whole of one's life is brought to mind in the name. When we hear the name Moses, those who have some biblical knowledge hear in an instant: baby in the bulrushes, prince of Egypt, murderer, stutterer, burning bush, manna, Commandments, and even his wistful watching as Joshua led the people across the Jordan to the next stage of God's promise. Having all of one's life and journey brought to mind in a name can be both good and daunting. One of the reasons that my husband left New York, where he grew up, was because he would always be Rob, just as he was at fifteen, there. He took a nickname for many years because he didn't want that rebellious teenager to define the adult man.

Names are built on relationship and they can be rebuilt as a result of relationship too. Years ago, when I worked at our denomination's headquarters, I had an acquaintance who worked in our mail room. We were just passing acquaintances who shared a smile or a joke whenever I was in her area. She seemed like such a sunny open person until one day she didn't anymore. It was like clouds had taken up residence in her eyes. She seemed veiled — polite, but there was no more twinkle. To my chagrin, I never asked anything more than how are you, to which she always looked down and said, "Fine." This went on for some time. Then one morning I arrived to pick up the mail and she was all smiles again. I told her that I had noticed things seemed off for a while and that now she was "back." I asked what had happened.

"I changed my name," she said with a broad smile.

"Oh," I said. "To what?"

"Mary Margaret," she said. "Mary is my first name and Margaret is my last name. I chose it myself."[2]

"Wow," I said. "How did you come to decide on that?"

"Well," she said, "I was abused by my father from the age of three and by my husband from the age of eighteen. I am finished with men's names. Margaret is my grandmother's name. She is the one who has shown me love and it is her name that I want to carry." Names have meanings and history.

In the Bible, names also carry the authority of a person. To do something in someone's name is to act for that one. It is like an ambassador for a country. When the ambassador speaks, it is the country speaking. Where the ambassador lives, anywhere in the world, she lives on the land of the home country. What one does in "the name" is the named one doing it.

It is incumbent on human beings to use each other's names carefully. The way we use a name can create a reality that sticks. If a name is said with an eyeroll, intentionally mispronounced, or instantly forgotten, that misuse distorts the truth and damages relationship.

In the summer of 2020, in addition to facing down COVID-19 and dealing with economic hardship, we faced a reckoning of centuries-long, deeply entrenched racism. One of the rallying calls of that moment was to say aloud the names of those who have been killed by police violence. It is a long list. When we say those names — Breonna, Rayshard, Tamir, Freddie, Ahmaud, George, and so many others — things begin to change inside us. I'm writing today on the fifth anniversary of the massacre at Mother Emanuel Church in Charleston, South Carolina. I remember vividly how, on the following Sunday in worship, we lit candles, as was our habit after mass casualty shootings. As the candles were lit, we repeated the names aloud. It was a breathlessly sacred moment. When we say the name, numbers become people, people become stories, and stories can be shared. To refuse to say a name is to erase a person and stop their story from moving forward. To dismiss or trivialize the name perpetuates the crime.

If designations of respect are dropped in situations of power imbalance, that itself can be a weapon. I remember once being introduced to a businessman in a community meeting. He was someone whose business had a foundation to which our church had submitted a grant application. When I was introduced to him, he said, "What do I call you? Preacherette?" In that name, he attempted to put me in a subordinate position, where he wanted me to stay, with him holding power and me rendered ridiculous.

The names we are called often have lasting consequences. They can take up residence in our minds and we find that we internalize their messages. If we are told that we are fat, old, useless, the problem, or any number of other names, we can find that we come to think that those names define us. The names we carry internally shape both our self-esteem and our moral choices. It has been a long time since I was called "Preacherette," but typing the word, I can still feel its impact in my body.

The Power of the Divine Name

In using God's name, the same dynamics hold and are magnified. The divine name of God, YHWH, revealed to Moses at the burning bush, carries the essence, power, and history of who God is. To share the Name was a gift of intimacy. To share the Name gives the person with whom the Name is shared a measure of power over the one who gives the gift.

According to this biblical mindset, God puts Godself on the line by sharing God's name with us. When God gives us the Name, somehow, mysteriously, we then have the capacity to wound God, to break God's heart, to misuse our intimacy and God's love. We may resist this idea, but all we have to do is look to Jesus and his sacrifice for love on the cross to see that God has always been willing to hurt God's own self in order to stay close to us.

The divine name, YHWH, was considered too holy to speak aloud in Bible times. It still is in many circles today. They might say *ha shem* (the name) or *Adonai* (Lord) instead. In English translations of Scripture, the name is rendered as Lord, in small caps, to signify this special treatment. The name means something like "Being Itself." Some have suggested that the word mimics the sound of the inflow and outflow of breath. The very sound of YHWH is considered an ecstasy. To speak it at all, even in the depths of one's heart, conjures up the whole of the story of God's work with God's people. It is all there in the one magnificent name.

To speak the Name at all is an act of intimacy that releases into our lives and world all that the Name contains. People who use God's name have a responsibility to uphold God's reputation, and, as we saw in Word Two, to make the relationship with God primary and not trivial.

The word we translate as "wrongful use" or "in vain" means to empty something of content, to make irrelevant, to misuse or make false. It refers to making something into nothing or to disappoint the hope it rests upon. It can also be translated as mischief, to make mischief with.

So far in the Words, God has chosen us and reminded us that God's deepest will is our release from bondage into an eternal love story. God has asked us not to look elsewhere for freedom and to embrace God's love fully without making idols of anyone or anything.

In Word Three, God says, don't make a mere idol of me either. Do not make me irrelevant, useless rubbish. Do not empty my name of its content. Do not use my name falsely. Do not abuse our relationship by attaching my name to things that are essentially contrary to it. To do so is a moral evil with consequences that will not be easily reversed.

The German writer and statesman Johan Wolfgang von Goethe (1749–1832) said,

> People treat the name of God as if that incomprehensible and most high Being, who is beyond the reach of human thought, were just another trivial thing. Otherwise they would not say, "Oh God," "for the love of God," "good God," and other such comments. These expressions become an empty phrase for most people, a barren name to which no thought is attached. If people were impressed by the sublime greatness of God, they would be silent; honor would keep them from mentioning God's name hardly at all.[3]

It doesn't take much reflection to see how making God's name a mindless expression of disbelief, astonishment, horror or excitement can, over time, render God's name, and then God, meaningless. Each use of God's name is a prayer, whether we intend it as such or not. This is especially problematic when we use God's name, not to bless others, but to curse them. When we use God's name to damn another, that will not, of course, affect the eternal disposition of their souls. It does, however, do violence to the relationship that is difficult or impossible to reverse. Even if we are using the curse without conscious thought, as an expression of frustration or befuddlement, it has the power to set things in motion. If what it sets in motion is only the inability to experience reverence or holiness, the toll is a powerful one, both on the speaker and the hearer. It does not take long for language such as this to cease to scandalize and God's immanent presence to slip from consciousness.

Maimonides, a physician and Torah scholar who lived 800 years ago, put it this way:

> Cursing is prohibited not because of what it can do to the victim, but because of its effect on the individual who pronounces it. Jewish law seeks to keep the individual from acquiring the damaging habit of ventilating anger and frustration on others.[4]

The misuse of the Name affects both the divine relationship and the human ones who are the receivers of our curse.

It's All about Relationship

There is more here than asking that the name of God be honored and rightly used in speech. This Word asks that the entirety of our relationship with God be honored and authentic. God does not wish to be taken for granted and knows that when we do that we have the capacity to block the flow of transforming love in our lives.

When we take God for granted, hoping God will be present when needed in the predictable ways we desire, and then at other times place God on a shelf far from our minds, practice, and principles, that is a powerful misuse of the Name. We then can compartmentalize our lives, with God for Sundays or times of trouble and our other priorities in charge for the rest of the time.

When I was raising money for our church's new homeless shelter, I sat next to an acquaintance at our weekly Kiwanis club luncheon. He was a wealthy and influential man in the city, and I hoped he would make a significant contribution to our work. I knew him to be an active leader in his church. Over our salads, I told him about our project. I shared the difficult circumstances of the guests in our basement shelter and how we believed we were all neighbors, beloved by God and worthy of care and concern. He put up his hand and said, "Eugenia, I'm a Christian, all right. But you are talking Sunday stuff. This is Tuesday. You are talking money and money is for business and not for Sundays." He had managed rather dramatically to put God in a box to have a claim on his life and resources only at certain times and in certain areas. He used God's name when and how it fit his other priorities.

Lest you find yourself shocked and shaking your head, as I did that day, we all do this to one degree or another. Often we use the potent idols of wealth or time or chasing our desires to put God in a box. A parishioner once told me that she always wrote out her bills at the kitchen table so she wouldn't have to look at the cross hanging over her library desk when she saw her true priorities reflected each month in her spending. When we claim to the world that God is there for us but do not live as if we are there for God, it is a misuse of the Name.

The Hebrew word we translate as "take" in take in vain, means to raise up, lift, bear, carry, wear, or apply to. The biblical writer recognizes the danger of applying God's name to things in a vain, frivolous, or self-serving way. We sometimes do this when we add "In God's name" to the close of prayers as if it is a magic potion that will guarantee that we get what we want regardless of whether or not that thing has any connection to God's will and values.

It is appropriate to pray in God's name when we are praying for the highest good of all involved. It is less appropriate to use the Name as a kind of talisman rendering our prayers more transactional than transformative. This is especially problematic because it can lead us to be convinced that something we want is really God's will. "In your name, I claim that Mercedes." "In your name, make him love me." "In your name, bring the prize patrol to my house." If the outcome we desire fails to materialize, we can become ever more desperate or disillusioned and our deep intimacy with God can get rocked.

Misusing the Name

We do this in deeper ways than a glib "OMG" in a text with our friends. One of the most damaging ways to mis-use God's name is to attach it to values, positions, or preju-dices that are antithetical to God's own being. When the KKK burns a cross, that is both blasphemy and a misuse of the Name. When preachers extolled the virtues of slavery in times past, or uphold racial stereotypes today, that is an obvious misuse of the name.

It can be wilier than that. When we claim that God is always and completely on our side theologically or ideo-logically, we not only misuse the Name, but put ourselves in a position where we cannot learn from each other's per-spectives or have our own limitations of understanding challenged. When we claim that God is on the side of our political opinions and therefore is not on the side of those who espouse a different view, we are on dangerous ground and perpetuate a dualism that is unknown to God and keeps us stuck and entrenched. The apostle Paul tells us in 1 Corinthians 13 that we see through a glass dimly, even when we look at ourselves and our own motives. Maybe especially then. When we presume to speak for God and of God, the Third Word encourages us to be humble and never to use God's name to manipulate others to do something that is just our preference or is not in their long-term best interest.

Early in the coronavirus pandemic, a pastor in a neighboring state made the news by declaring that he did not care about the safety guidelines, he was holding church services no matter what. He did. More than a thousand congregants gathered, sitting cheek by jowl, hugging and worshiping for a couple of hours at a time. When asked why he was defying state orders, he said, that his people were not "wussies." They were washed in the blood of Jesus and therefore no virus threatened them. Furthermore, if someone's faith was weak and they did get it, then the church was giving out healing handkerchiefs that would immediately break the virus' hold.

Now granted, that is not my theology and so I was predisposed to become enraged and shamefully judgmental when I read this. This pastor's response was utterly heartfelt, just as mine was to his. Still, in my view, this kind of action treats God like a circus act and assumes that human beings can convince God, with a handkerchief or anything else, to balance a beach ball on his nose! To assume that God will contravene God's own laws of physics for a special few who believe hard enough is enough to make me want to run through the streets screaming. To use God's name in this way not only put people's lives in danger (the church became a viral hotspot), it was also cruel. Using God's name in this way left those who fell ill believing that their illness was either punishment for sin or their own lack of faith. It even left them as willing, if unwitting, executioners of their friends and people in the community they did not even know. Even our most heartfelt acts of faith must always pass the love test before we attach God's name to them. God's name is not to be used to wound or to support our need to feel right or superior.

This is, of course, not new to the coronavirus outbreak. During the height of the AIDS epidemic, some pastors in the community where I then served took out ads in the newspaper claiming that AIDS was incompatible with the Christian faith, was a punishment from God, and no persons with it, or their families, were welcomed in their churches. To this they attached the name of God fervently, no doubt, believing that they were doing the right thing. Still, when we attach God's name as a for-all-time-authority to our own partial understandings, we make powerful mischief with the Name. Who knows how many lost faith or hope in a God like that.

How we use God's name, what we attach it to, and the content with which we fill the Name, tell the world who we think that God is. If we use the Name too casually, we tell the world God doesn't mean much. If we use the Name as a weapon on others, they can wind up cringing before God like puppies kicked too many times. If we use the Name arrogantly, assuming that God is for and against everything and everybody we are for and against, we make enemies with the Name rather than fostering the beloved community for which we were created. God, then, is little more than a useful tactic or a trivial afterthought.

Cursing the Name

The book of Job pushes us further to think about what circumstances could lead us to curse God. The book does not merely focus on the mystery of why good people suffer if God is all powerful and completely just. There is a deeper issue: what will it take to cause a person of faith to curse and give up on God? Is pain enough? Is injustice enough? Are grief and loss enough?

A former parishioner of mine, a gifted and loving young man, posted a comment of such despair on Facebook recently that it took my breath away. He said that he just gave up, that injustice would kick justice's butt every day and twice on Sunday. He said he had concluded that there is no arc in the moral universe bending inexorably toward justice.

What took him to that point? For him it was another killing of an unarmed black man by police officers. What might it be for you? At what point might you do what Job would not, curse God and die?

I had a spate of suicides in my congregation once—five within a year. We were roiled by this, and it took a toll on all of us. These were faithful, loving people. Yet their different pain and demons overwhelmed them to the point that they could see no hope, no way through except out. I remember one of them, a man in his fifties, saying to me in a rambling, drunken phone call, "Why does God hate me? I'm coming to hate him too." I tried to listen. I tried to reassure. I tried to guide. I tried to refer. Looking back, though, I wonder if, in my desperation to find a way to redirect him from the precipice, in my fatigue with his constant need, I trivialized his pain and God in the process. I'm not sure. A month later he was dead.

How do we speak the name of God when people are in the deepest pain without either trivializing them, or God, or both? How do we use God's name in ways that uplift and do not inflict greater pain?

Our discomfort with our own and others' hardships has given rise to many platitudes that we turn to as life rafts.

When a loved one dies, we say to the bereaved things like, "God just needed another angel in heaven." Or "It was God's will." Or "We mustn't question God." Each of those statements subtly judges the hurting person for his feelings and sets God up as the enemy who caused it all.

The issue that Job raises in light of the Third Word is how do we talk about God in a hurting world in such a way that God is not trivialized? One of my friends, who lost her son the week after he graduated from college, told me later that when it all happened she could not bear to hear God spoken of at all. The only thing anyone said to her that really mattered to her was when a friend said, "This just sucks." She said those words were God speaking to her, and all the other well-meaning words felt like battering rams. Sometimes, God speaks when we do not utter the Name more powerfully and helpfully than when we do. Silence, after all, is God's first language.

Sometimes, we can vainly use God's name to shield our ego's games. In counseling, it is often a clue that someone is lying to you, or themselves, when she says, "I swear to God." These games can be hard to spot in ourselves. When the false self is firmly in charge of how we see ourselves, we can think that our masks and roles are all that there is to us. We can believe and live our own lies. In Tolstoy's short story, *Father Sergius*, at one point the priest cries out, "I lived for men on the pretext of living for God."

When we are strangers to ourselves, how can we be intimate with God? We may do good things. We may do them in the name of God. People may even be blessed and helped by them, such is God's goodness and faithfulness. What rarely happens, though, is transformation of our deep hearts such that, more and more, we come to embody God's love and therefore speak God's name with winsome authority.

It was that capacity to speak of God apart from ego manipulations and false self that led those around Jesus to marvel at him and the authority with which he spoke. As we grow in our own healing journeys, authentic and faithful ways of speaking of God become natural. They flow from us because they are in us and no longer obscured by unexamined neediness or shoved down pain. We become more obviously who we are. We begin to look more like the body of Christ. Our witness wounds less and our words heal more.

Dare We Speak?

We know, as the apostle Paul says, that we live in an already-and-not-yet time. We are already whole, saved, perfected in Christ. We are simultaneously broken, selfish, and rarely live for extended periods of time without ego's dramatic pull. Knowing that, how do we talk about God at all? Do we dare? With what words do we describe God? What words do we use in worship for God? How do we use God's name?

The Scriptures themselves give us a myriad of images with which we can speak of God. Some of these metaphors have been overused and have come, painfully for some, to define God, rather than to open the heart by pointing to God. The image of God as Father, so rich and beautiful and evocative of protection, source, and identity in the Bible, can, through less-than-mindful use, leave vulnerable people seeing God through the lens of their own fathers. In Scripture, the image of God as judge is one of truth telling and opportunity to reform. Many today see it more as an image of destruction and rejection that reinforces deep shame. It keeps the false self firmly in control and dampens the desire to draw close to God at all. Biblical images of God as feminine can cause some people, who insist that God is actually male, to light their hair on fire and run screaming heresy, while others find that they can finally breathe again. The problem comes when we concretize images and metaphors that are given to us as ways to enter into intimacy with God, and think that they contain the totality of God in exactly the way we understand it. We then tend to use God as an opportunity to draw lines in the sand and claim that some are right and others are wrong. There is no opportunity then for conversation that may open all of us to deeper truth and understanding. This is a misuse of the Name.

In addition to waking up to the ways you may misuse the Name, think about the worthy ways that you can address God. What adjectives and metaphors to describe God are meaningful to you right now? How might you speak Divine Love into your life, family, and community? Are your friends or family members ill, afraid, or grieving? Have people you know taken a hard financial hit lately? How might the love of God be spoken with reverence and gentleness into those situations? Remember that God lives inside of you. You are a temple. When you speak, you represent God to the world. How do you choose to speak of and for God?

Conclusion

As you reflect on the Third Word, you may realize that you have slipped into a habitual pattern of trivializing God and misusing the Name. Many of us have. We are like the little child in the opening of this chapter, running around using God's name to carry a whole variety of emotions while never thinking of God at all. God's name is never frivolous. No use of it is ever really meaningless. When we trivialize the Name, we empty it of its power to lift, heal, and connect us.

If you feel the need to confess your sorrow to God for taking God for granted, do that. If you are like me, this may become a frequent prayer. Ask God to help you change your habit from misuse to new intimacy. As you honor the Name, God will also honor you with more of who God really is. This is a big responsibility. Be careful with it.

Spiritual Practice: Silence

If you feel overwhelmed or befuddled by the Third Word, take some time to practice the ancient spiritual discipline of silence. Rather than addressing God at all, or assaulting the throne of heaven with your needs, desires, or intercessions, just close your eyes and breathe. As with breath prayer, don't be concerned with your leaping thoughts. As they come up, let them pass without judgment or attaching too much weight to them. If they are important, they will return at a more appropriate time. Sit in silence, close your eyes. In the silence, imagine that you are opening your heart up to God. Just opening, not explaining, not defending. Just you, opening to Divine Love. Sit in openness and allow love to flow. This will happen whether you know it or not. Something will begin to shift inside you. You may not notice it for weeks or months but one day it will be apparent.

If this is hard, return to your breath prayer: (breathe in) "I am," (breathe out) "Yours." This time, rather than breathing the phrase in and out as before, see it in letters across the dark of your closed eyes. Don't focus on the letters. Focus on the space between the letters. For a split second that space may seem to stretch out to eternity and be filled with Presence. Just sit with that space and that Presence. You may find that you cry in this time. No need to analyze or stop the tears. I sometimes tell people that tears are a natural reminder of the power of our baptism. Simply let yourself be in the holiness of God's presence in silence.

Questions for Personal and Group Reflection

1. In what ways do you see God's name trivialized in our day? How do you think the mindless use of God's name affects how the culture views God?
2. What criteria do you use to decide if God's name should be applied to something? Be specific.
3. Have you ever thought you were speaking the truth of God or about God and later realized that you were wrong? What did you learn from that?
4. How might you help your family or church recover a sense of reverence for God?
5. Do you find that you use the name of God lightly, without thinking or reverence? When is that most likely?
6. Do you ever hear platitudes that upon examination could be harmful or hurtful? Do you have a story to share about an instance when this happened?

CHAPTER 4

JUST STOP

Addressing Toxic Doing

Remember the sabbath day, and keep it holy. Six days you shall labor and do all your work. But the seventh day is a sabbath to the LORD *your God; you shall not do any work —you, your son or your daughter, your male or female slave, your livestock, or the alien resident in your towns. For in six days the* LORD *made heaven and earth, the sea, and all that is in them, but rested the seventh day; therefore the* LORD *blessed the sabbath day and consecrated it.*

—Exodus 20:8–11

My mother is 95 years old. She grew up in central Florida during the Great Depression. Her parents were Scottish immigrants who settled in Florida via a circuitous route. My grandmother, who died when my mom was eleven, was a pillar of the local Presbyterian church. She was an old school Scots Presbyterian who took the living out of her faith seriously and strictly. Scones and warm oat cakes awaited my mom when she scampered home from school after stopping and poking sticks at the edges of the beautiful lakes, hoping to rise a fat toad or find a flower on the many lily pads. She loved it.

Sundays were different though. Sunday school and church were OK. It was Sunday afternoons that were difficult. My mother reports the agony of sitting on the porch watching the other children scampering to the lake to swim or fish, while she sat next to her mom who spent the afternoon reading her Bible, the Psalms mostly, and refused to allow the children to so much as thread a needle.

For my hardworking, Depression-weary grandmother, Sundays were bliss. There was no housework. The food had already been prepared. My grandfather was home and somehow entertaining the boys. She could sit, sip tea, and become herself again.

For my mother, though, it was a joyless exercise in teeth-gritting discipline. She hated it. She hated that strictly disciplined approach in her heritage so much that when I came home and told her that I felt called to be a Presbyterian pastor, she cried all afternoon. All she could see stretching before me was an endless stream of "thou shalt nots" while the joyous romp of life went on without me. Have we somehow missed the mark in our teaching of Sabbath blessing?

The Fourth Word serves as an important link between the first three Words and those that follow. The first three Words urge us to examine our personal relationship with God, the blocks to it and the ways we trivialize it. Words five through ten invite us to consider how we live *together* once we are rooted in our love story with God. The Fourth Word links personal practice with community piety to help us understand that our love story is not exclusively personal. It is always lived out in community. In the same way, worship is not essentially personal.

Sabbath teaches us that life has a rhythm. It moves and it slows. It rises and it falls away. It hurries and it stops.

There is work and there is rest. That rhythm is baked into the created order itself and is in the very nature of God. Our biblical ancestors knew that all of life was defined by these rhythms. Sabbath was such a touchstone of life that days were counted by it. It is two days until Sabbath. It is six days until Sabbath.

After the wild burst of creation, God stopped, observed, rested, and simply was. If human beings are to mirror God on earth, as beings created in God's image, then stopping, observing, resting, and being are necessary. We are made for it. Yet, of all of the Words, this one has been the hardest for me to live.

When I was pastor of First Presbyterian Church in Birmingham, Alabama, my staff and I took a day of prayer together most months. On those days, we showed up at the big old downtown church in jeans and T-shirts, piled into somebody's car, and headed north from the city for about an hour's drive to a lovely small Benedictine convent where we spent the day. We prayed together in the morning, ate lunch with the sisters, and had quiet time in the afternoons.

One day, one of the sisters with whom I had sought spiritual direction a time or two stopped me in a quiet hallway. "Reverend Eugenia," she said, "just stop." At first I didn't know what she meant. Was I wearing my Protestantism like a giant, scarlet P and doing something offensive? Was I walking too fast, too loudly, too something? I stopped and looked at her, confused. "When was the last time you took even five minutes of Sabbath?" she asked. "When was the last time you just stopped?" I stood there frozen. I could not remember the last time I had simply stopped.

There is not much in our culture that supports Sabbath. Often, we are applauded for our busyness, our fast-paced schedules, our many responsibilities. In the flurry of overtime at work, ferrying the kids to games and classes, or volunteering at church, the idea of "just stopping" seems beyond us. My daughter-in-law, a speech therapist and mother of five- and three-year-old girls, says that her idea of Sabbath is being able to go to the bathroom by herself! I get that.

A Palace in Time

It is difficult to express the importance and the vitality of Sabbath to our faith ancestors. Some ancient rabbis even taught that Messiah would come if Israel kept two holy Sabbaths. The word sabbath means "to stop" or "to cease." Sabbath stopping is always purposeful. It is for the purpose of reorienting all of life toward God and in the presence of God. The rabbis taught that even the air smelled different on Sabbath. Tastes were sweeter and more pungent. Laughter was more full-throated and rest more restorative.

Sabbath is not just a pious word for Sunday. It is not simply stopping work. Sabbath is about regularly stopping our habitual doing in order to reorient life in the presence of and toward the values of God. The rabbis called Sabbath a "palace in time" because when we keep Sabbath, we leave this world and actually enter into the vastness and wonder of eternity.

On Sabbath we acknowledge, by our stopping and careful attention, that, just as it is in heaven, all is as it should be on earth as well. God is at work and will provide. We become more aware on Sabbath that life has meaning, holiness, and purpose.

When we worship together on Sabbath and celebrate the sacrament of Holy Communion, we share, at that Table, in the great eternal banquet. As the elements are lifted up for us, we are gathered into God's cosmic celebration with all of those who have gone before us and all who will come after us. We leave this world, while still planted firmly in it, and breathe in the air of eternity. When we break bread, pour the cup, and share, we are gathered up into Divine Love in all its fullness.

This is not something that is accomplished by our doing, even with our cherished rituals. Communion is accomplished by God. We show up for it. We stop to receive it. We make room for the sacred as we pray and consecrate. We receive the fullness of God's presence. When we do that we enter into the palace in time.

Rabbi Abraham Heschel tells a Jewish rabbinic legend that makes this point beautifully. Students ask their teacher, "Show us in this world an example of the world to come. The Sabbath is an example of the world to come."[1]

Sabbath-keeping connects us with eternity and humbles us enough to experience our lives, and eternal life, as blessing. When we stop our constant doing, and orient ourselves toward God, we find that everything is really a gift in the first place. Our hearts beat. Our lungs breathe. Our blood flows. All of that without our asking. The sun rises. The sun sets. We do not control it. Seasons come and go apart from our willing them.

Granted, there are times when we do damage to the earth's and our own natural cycles and restorative powers. Still, those cycles are enormously resilient. During the time of coronavirus lockdown, the canals in Venice cleared. Birds were heard singing in cities that had not heard birds for years. Rivers and wildlife began to recover from constant neglect and misuse. We, with all of our doing, did not make that happen. By our stopping, it was allowed to happen.

When we know that everything is not up to us, that God actually is and can manage the universe for twenty-four hours without our doing anything, we begin to release the knots in our bodies and in our souls. Mature spiritual practice always involves release. We die to live. We let go in order to be held. Sabbath itself is something we release into, not something we master by sheer force of will.

In Sabbath-keeping, we recognize that we are not big enough to carry the world or even to fix our own problems. We are helpless to control others and not much good at controlling ourselves. We are helpless even to provide for ourselves ultimately or to ensure that we have another day.

When we keep Sabbath regularly and deeply over time, we practice relinquishment and begin to learn that we lose nothing by letting go. We let go into Love and are met by it. That does not make loss more tolerable, or the fear of change less fierce, but it does make trust easier to find over time. Sabbath helps us practice dependence and learn to trust God's provision. It also helps us to remember that we are a part of something much bigger and more durable than our small lives. We are a part of the sweep of eternal love. In Sabbath, we taste what we will fully live in eternity. Sabbath-keeping is about relinquishing not just the externals of our life's work, but also the ego's games and illusions of control and superiority. Only then does it become a palace in time and cease to be another set of practices for a scared and scarred ego to master.

Keeping the Rules

Trying to wrestle Sabbath into a list of rules inevitably leads to resentment. The day becomes all about us getting our fun, or rest, our family time, or simply not being responsible for what we don't want to be responsible for in the first place.

Sabbath-keeping is about letting go of ordinary daily life in order to experience being truly alive as God intends. It is not about letting go for the sake of letting go. Nor is it accomplished by gritty obedience alone. When we make Sabbath solely about keeping the rules, and focus on our ability or inability to abide by them, it loses its sacred mystery. It ceases to become a gift and becomes a burden.

We have struggled with this for centuries. By the time Jesus lived, specific instructions for Sabbath-keeping were codified into law. These laws were never intended to obscure the celebration, rest, and honoring of God that lay at Sabbath's heart. They were intended to help people learn how to do that celebrating and to identify what would get in their way. Over time, Sabbath came to focus largely on abstinence from work. Thirty-nine classes of prohibited work are listed in the Mishnah, a collection of Jewish oral law dating to about 200 CE. Religious authorities took these lists very seriously and were vigilant in patrolling them.

Jesus often extended the boundaries of Sabbath observance and got in trouble for it every time. In Mark 2, after allowing his disciples to pluck a few grains to eat as they passed through a field, Jesus is confronted by the authorities. In that encounter, Jesus appeals to an incident recorded in 1 Samuel 21, in which King David convinces the priests to give consecrated bread to his hungry soldiers. In closing his debate with the authorities, Jesus says, "The sabbath was made for humankind and not humankind for the sabbath" (Mark 2:27). In other words, Sabbath is intended to serve humans' lives and relationship with God, not to become a legalistic burden.

In a sense, legalism itself can be a violation of Sabbath-keeping. Legalism places the priority on human action and interpretation making Sabbath-keeping a work. Doing that throws the responsibility for Sabbath right back on human doing rather than on sacred restoration.

Of course, there is an element of human will and choice in keeping Sabbath. The text of the Words in Exodus tells us to "remember" Sabbath and to keep it holy. Remembering invites us to pause and bring to mind the stories of God's creative activity. Remembering is rooted in the celebration of creation and of relationship with God.

Sabbath-remembering is not just recalling what day it is. It is recalling to whom all days belong. The healing of Sabbath comes when we remember God's goodness, provision, and promise. On Sabbath we are asked to remember the moments God has touched our awareness and the miracles of love that we can see only looking back. Sabbath-remembering asks us to recall and rehearse the stories of God's activity in human life from the beginning to today. Refraining from work is not about stopping for its own sake. It is about focus that has the power to change the future.

Sabbath and the True Self

In addition, Sabbath encourages us to see not only who God is and all that God has done and does. It encourages us to see anew who we are in our deepest selves and how that self is defined in relationship to God.

Often, all of our doing and achieving anesthetizes us to our real selves so effectively, that we don't know who we are apart from what we do. As a recently retired pastor, my neglect of this aspect of Sabbath became painfully clear. Without the weekly sermons, the studies, the planning meetings, the calls for care, I wondered if there was really a Eugenia at all.

If we do not accept the gift of Sabbath routinely over time, we will have to face the deficits that result from that neglect one way or another. It has taken me the better part of a year to dig through a little of the muck left behind by rarely stopping to just be me with God, without agenda. It has required painfully letting go of roles that can so easily substitute for a self and befriending the parts of myself that I had pushed to the side and did not want to look at.

Sabbath is designed to help us routinely and regularly look at, and live into, who God made us, with all of our gifts and imperfections. Sabbath reminds us that we are who we are, and God is who God is. We are encouraged every week to get that equation right side up instead of upside down.

The inner "work" of Sabbath is hard if long neglected. It is hard if neglected at all. It is essential work, however. When we dedicate time to God for Sabbath, we place ourselves in God's hands to both redeem and reveal the inner lies and delusions that can secretly cripple our lives, hurt others, and leave us feeling fractured and frantic.

Sabbath-keeping includes accepting God's forgiveness, then forgiving ourselves for the choices, steps, and missteps we have taken that have led us to where we currently are. We can only find God's rest when we see ourselves clearly. Sabbath includes the healing work of ceasing to blame others for our circumstances and emotional states. Reorienting self and all of life to God makes it much more difficult to project our wounds or our ideas of what is right and what we need to be happy onto others who simply cannot provide what we deeply need.

A Time for Unlearning

The inner work of Sabbath is about unlearning as well as learning. Sabbath invites us to unlearn the lies that tell us we are only valuable for what we do or produce. It invites us to unlearn the habits of mind that stoke our fears, frustrations, and exhaustion. It invites us to unlearn the repeated patterns of living and thinking that we have all developed to soothe a wound or quiet a fear. Sabbath invites us to lay aside the "musts," the "shoulds," and the "oughts" of our daily lives for a while, to feel what it is like to release those things into God's care for a time and just be.

A part of unlearning includes releasing toxic judgments that keep us wrapped in a cycle of narcissistically trying to control others or castigate ourselves. It is nearly impossible to rest, renew, experience God, and do the inner work of Sabbath if our minds are obsessed with judging other people as either wrong or right, better or worse, than ourselves. Those judgments are a part of the burden that Sabbath asks us to relinquish.

Toxic judging is no less damaging when aimed at ourselves as when aimed at others. If all we think of when we stop working is all that we haven't done or didn't do well, or if we ruminate on the fact that we feel like we are basically frauds or failures as parents, spouses, friends, church members, or human beings, we will know no rest ever. To enter into the healing of Sabbath, we must choose to let those thoughts go, give them no energy, and find within ourselves the wellspring of compassion that sitting in God's presence inevitably reveals.

God reminds us in the Fourth Word that before we can live rightly in community we must learn to live rightly with God and ourselves. Sabbath invites us to lay aside our doing to commune with God as we are. In so doing, we find, not only more of God, but more of who we are at the deepest levels. It is a tough journey to unhook and unmask. Still, even the air smells different when we do.

The Gifts of Sabbath-Keeping

Sabbath-keeping includes many gifts! In it, relaxation takes on new meaning. No longer is it creating time and space for activities that we enjoy, as wonderful and nourishing as those things are. It is doing those things wide awake, full of God's presence and gratitude for life itself. The difference between self-care and Sabbath is awareness of God. It is doing what we do, with and for God whose temple we each are.

Perhaps the most surprising gift of Sabbath-keeping is its radical declaration of justice. In Sabbath, in the entire Ten Words really, God gives us a picture of what we look like healed, what God's vision for a new earth and heaven looks like. In declaring that Sabbath applies equally to all people, and even to the animals, God reminds us that there is no person, no part of the created order, that is outside the flow of God's healing love. The rest of Sabbath does not apply only to the faithful or the dominant. It applies to women and men equally, slave and free equally. All people, and all of creation, are called into the rest of God's reorienting presence, without exception.

The radical equality of Sabbath is demonstrated by the fact that no one works that day. (Exod. 20:10 makes explicit that slaves and aliens in the land are to be included in Sabbath's joys and rest.) When no one works no one has more. No one is in charge of another. No one dictates the status of another. All are equally and totally dependent upon God. This is the kingdom of heaven into which Sabbath invites us to release every week. When we do that, we naturally take that vision into the way we live and work throughout the rest of the week. On Sabbath we live in justice to strengthen us to work for justice.

As profound as this aspect of Sabbath is, we must be mindful of the ways that privilege complicates our practice. For example, if, as a Sabbath practice, we decide not to cook and to take the family out to eat at a restaurant after church, we then force others to work in order to support our stopping. Sabbath rest cannot be paid for on the backs of others' labor.

To keep Sabbath fully requires a radical paradigm shift. Sabbath invites us into a revolution in which the old worldview of constant work, of hierarchy and domination, is revealed as shabby and so torn it can no longer be mended. As Jesus put it, the old wine skins cannot hold the new wine. The transformation that takes place on Sabbath is not simply the release of that which binds so that we can take a deep breath again. It is the experience of justice itself.

Sabbath Justice

Recently, a telling meme went around the internet trying to help people understand the differences between equality, equity, and justice. In the first frame two young boys were standing facing a wooden fence that separates them from a baseball game that they want to watch. One of the boys is older and taller than the other. Neither can see the game. Both are shut out, without access. This frame is labeled "injustice."

The second frame shows the same two boys. This time each has been given an equal-sized box to stand on. The taller boy can now see over the fence but the smaller one still can't. This frame is labeled equality. Each was given the same leg up.

In the third frame, the taller boy still has his box, but the younger boy has two boxes to stand on. Both can now see the game. Each is given what each needs in order to have access. This frame is labeled "equity."

In the final frame, the wooden fence is taken down. Both boys stand on their own two feet, exactly as they are. The barrier to their access has been removed. This frame is labeled "justice." We have to be careful with illustrations like this not to allow it to imply that the smaller boy did not have access because of an inherent characteristic in himself. The problem was not with the boys. The problem was the fence.

Biblical justice is always about removing the barriers to access to the fullness of life and the flow of God's love. It is not about punishment. That is retribution. Nor is it about people getting what they somehow have earned or deserve. God's call to Sabbath gives us a picture of biblical justice as removing any barriers to access, any divisions of wealth, any hierarchies of privilege. Sabbath asks us to enter into that vision and be changed by it. Once we orient our lives toward God, once we see this vision, we cannot help but take it with us. Nothing else will ever feel right again.

Sabbath, by design, addresses injustice and its consequences at every level. Endless work on the top and on the bottom creates violence. It does not escape my notice today that I am writing this chapter on Juneteenth, the observance of the day in 1865 that the word of the emancipation proclamation reached the last slave communities in Texas. Protests and celebrations continue to fill the headlines today. I am reminded of a quote attributed to the Southern writer William Faulkner, "The past is not dead. It is not even past." Sabbath is a gift to help us see rightly. When practiced, it strengthens us to do and be what we see.

Sabbath practice asks us to keep God's vision for justice front and center, to make the experience of it a touchstone for our lives every week so that, as God remakes each of us on Sabbath, God can then use us to transform a hurting world that has organized itself around lesser gods.

Sabbath justice takes place not only in our personal Sabbath experience but in worship as well. A few years ago I attended a preaching seminar led by the Rev. Dr. James Forbes, pastor emeritus of the Riverside Church in New York City.[2] I remember vividly him saying, "Worship without social justice is just a lie seeking a microphone." Yes, it is.

In a society that never stops, where consuming is what keeps the economy afloat and few stores close one day a week, the idea of stopping for a day of reorientation, celebration, self-awareness, and justice is not just rejected, it is unthinkable.

This is especially problematic for those who have the least and are most vulnerable in society. How do we encourage Sabbath in a world of injustice without creating more injustice? To ask a person who will not eat for a day if she doesn't work that day to cease just increases the inequity. In a society that does not keep Sabbath, how do we prevent the gift itself from being just another blessing for the already privileged? This struggle is as old as time. Jesus and his followers wrestled with it. To keep the law, must we go hungry? Jesus said no.

In a society steeped in a scarcity mentality, convinced that there is never enough so one can never stop acquiring in order to feel safe enough to sleep at night, how do we teach and practice Sabbath stopping, releasing, and reordering?

It goes against everything we know of God to imagine that Sabbath is only a gift for the favored few. It goes against the Scripture itself. It goes against everything we know of God to imagine an instruction that would make a bad situation worse for the vulnerable or make them feel that they could not access the grace of God due to circumstances over which they have little control. To deny the reality of injustice as the stew in which we try to practice Sabbath does nothing but allow us to be cruel while refusing to see it as cruelty.

Planting Seeds of Sabbath

So what do we do? We do the best we can. As tennis great Arthur Ashe once said, "Start where you are, use what you have, do what you can."[3] We all can encourage each other in this practice. If our circumstances don't seem to allow us to rest for a full day, perhaps we can begin with a moment, then fifteen minutes, then an hour, then two, then three. My experience is that the busier I am, the more I need to stop and pray. The more I stop and pray when I am busy, the less busy I become. Martin Luther once remarked that he was so busy one day that he needed to pray two hours instead of one. We start. We start by creating small stops and move to larger commitments. We have to be careful not to let the small stops become an excuse to not move deeply. Five minutes of Sabbath practice is not the same as a day. It is not worthless though, and will be used.

During the time of pandemic, I wondered if enforced stopping is the same as Sabbath. I decided it is not, but it does create space for it if we are open to the practice. Sabbath doesn't happen kicking and screaming. It is all about intention and making room for what really matters.

Perhaps we can start by planting seeds of Sabbath in our lives, families, and churches. When I was about seven years old, I found a business opportunity in a small advertisement in the back of *Highlights* magazine. The opportunity was to sell packets of seeds to earn points to get a Brownie instamatic camera. I was so excited I could hardly contain myself. I recruited my two older cousins to go into business with me. Visions of me walking to school with the little camera dangling from my wrist danced in my head.

When my seed packets arrived, I fell in love with the vibrant pictures on the packets, zinnias in all my favorite colors, fat cucumbers, and fluffy-topped carrots. My cousins decided that to improve our profits we should buy some seeds ourselves, plant a garden and then sell the produce to neighbors from our little red wagon.

With my business plan firmly in place, one Saturday afternoon I asked for advice from my father as he sat on the back porch enjoying the summer breeze. I spread the packets out on the little wicker table where he had his dripping glass of iced tea. I explained the plan and asked him which seeds he thought I should keep and plant.

"What do you like," he asked. I picked up a package with a picture of peonies on the front. He looked at it, turned it over, and read the back, then replied. "Be careful which seeds you plant so you get the garden that you want."

He was of course telling me that what thrives on the coast of Maine will not even sprout in south Alabama, but still. There was a deeper wisdom there than what he or I thought in that moment. Be careful the seeds you plant so that you will get the garden you want. (I eventually did sell enough seed packets to get my little camera—mostly, as I recall, to my father.)

What seeds of Sabbath might you plant? Take some time to ponder the following questions:

Will you plant a willingness to rest in God a little bit each day?

Will you make a commitment to ask God to help you know yourself in deeper ways?

Will you examine your reaction to the word "justice"?

Will you examine your heart and choose to release those commitments and habits of mind that block love's fullness in your life?

Will you stop and ponder Jesus' teaching that the way we treat others is the way we treat God? (Matthew 25)

Will you sit for a time with the world's sorrow, without judgment, blame, or agenda? Will you sit with the tears of God until they soften and change you utterly?

Will you open your eyes to beauty, give your plants
   a drink of water, kiss the soft fur of your sleeping
   pet?
Will you inspect your anger and look for the true
   source, offer that to God for healing, as a rich
   Sabbath treat?
Will you ponder what your calling might be for the
   other days and hours of your life?

Each commitment made and kept, each seed of Sabbath sown in yourself, your family, your church, will grow.
Transformed communities come into being when the per-
centage of transformed people reaches a tipping point.

Conclusion

Keeping Sabbath is not just about our worship life together,
as important as that practice is. In Sabbath-keeping, God
seeks to heal our tired and wounded bodies, minds, souls,
and systems. Sabbath is about letting go. It is about finding
self and God and others in a new way. It is about resting in
the vision of heaven and being strengthened to bring that
vision into the here and now. With this Word, God seeks to
restore our tired, fragmented hearts and re-create, in and
with us, a new community of love and holiness. When we
practice Sabbath, we mirror God who took Sabbath too.
We release into joy and let go of the stress of our constant,
often mindless, doing. When we grasp that we are beloved,
that God comes first, that we do not trivialize our relationship with God, and practice regular reorientation of all of
life toward God, then we are ready to turn our attention
to healing our communities. We will begin that journey in
chapter 5.

Spiritual Practice: Contemplative Prayer

Sabbath itself is a form of contemplative prayer in which we refuse to produce or perform and begin to see the bigness of God and how ephemeral our ego strivings really are.

Centering prayer is a form of contemplative prayer that is practiced in silence. The core of it is release. In brief, centering prayer is an ancient, sacred style of praying that is in some ways similar to meditation. The difference is that centering prayer is not about emptying or stilling the mind. That is not the point. The point is intention, the intention to present oneself as open and available to God. This availability is from the depths of ones being, your memories, emotions, desires, all of it. In centering prayer, you choose to give yourself, for this time, into the mystery of God's presence.

Your prayer can begin as simply as saying, "I am here." Tell yourself before your prayer time that if your mind races or you start planning or ruminating that you will call yourself back. To call yourself back it can be useful to use a sacred word that you choose. It could be Jesus, Spirit, Lord, or even a word that you make sacred by the way you use it, such as open or return. The word is not your prayer. It is a tool to help you return to openness in your prayer.

As you enter into your prayer time, be sure that you have an uninterrupted time and place. If you are unused to this type of prayer, it might be helpful to begin with a Scripture phrase to gather yourself in. I often use "Be still and know that I am God" from Psalm 46 (v. 10). Close your eyes and sit comfortably. Repeat the phrase three times slowly. Then repeat "Be still and know" three times. Then "Be still" three times and finally, "Be" three times. Then simply state your intention: I am here. Then sit in the Presence. To start, try this for about ten minutes.

Questions for Personal and Group Reflection

1. Before reading this chapter, what did you think the word Sabbath meant? Has anything changed for you now?
2. What, if anything, did you find most intriguing in the chapter? Why?
3. What do you see as the biggest obstacles to Sabbath practice in your life and community?
4. How does extending Sabbath practice to the vulnerable and the created order itself strike you? How might we do that?
5. How might you begin to deepen your practice of Sabbath?

CHAPTER 5

⚮

IT TAKES A "CRASH"

Addressing the Power of Family Pain

*Honor your father and your mother, so that your days may be long in
the land that the* LORD *your God is giving you.*

—Exodus 20:12

The Fifth Word marks a decisive shift in both the tone
and context of the Ten Words. With the Fourth Word,
we opened the door to a larger vision of our life with God
together. In the Fifth Word, we walk through that open door.
From this point on, the Hebrew language shifts from the
singular to the plural. God reveals to us what the beloved
community of God's children actually looks like. In it, those
things we are encouraged to do, like honor parents, are a
way of life. The things we are forbidden to do, simply do
not happen.

Norms for human life and interaction naturally begin
with the family. In the beloved community, life givers are
honored, and families are loving and stable. This is the only

one of the Ten Words that comes with a specific promise of blessing attached to the keeping of it.

Several years ago, while leading a retreat on the Ten Words, a young woman came up to me after my presentation of this Word. She was agitated, shaking so visibly that I thought her bones might disconnect from their joints. Her arms shook even though they were wrapped tightly around her torso. She looked wild, caged, hunted.

She told me how the critical voice of her mother plays across her mind constantly, like a breaking news scroll on the bottom of a newscast. She talked about the pain of this, giving example after example. When she was spent, she said, "How do I honor my mother without dishonoring me? How do I honor her when she is old and has not changed and there is not one thing that I will miss about her when she is gone?"

She took a deep breath and burst into tears. Through sobs she said, "What if my children feel the same way about me?" How do we answer this young woman's tearful question?

Every rule tells a story. By the time God offered this picture of family life to Moses and the people, Israel had a long history checkered with incidents of elder abuse and disrespect of parents. Lot's daughters got him drunk and raped him. Jacob tricked his feeble father into giving him Esau's birthright. Simeon and Levi tricked their father by murdering the clan of Shechem. Rachel dishonored Laban by stealing his household gods while claiming she was having her period to avoid being searched! Clearly, generational struggles for power, identity, and control are nothing new.

Interestingly, the text of this Word makes clear that it is addressed to adult children, not minors. It is not so simple as telling us to obey our parents when we are little so that we don't burn the house down or run out into traffic. Nor is this a Word that blithely tells us to love our parents and to take them out to dinner on Mother's or Father's Day.

The Hebrew word that we translate as "honor," *kabbed*, comes from the root word for "to fear" or "to revere." It means "to give something its due weight or importance." It does not mean to obey without question, although later rabbinic writings expanded this command to include general obedience. Neither does it mean to give undue, or excessive, weight to parents to the point of doing oneself damage. This Word is about giving parents a rightful and respectful place in life and in the community.

In a patriarchal society where men's words, stories, and worth were dominant and usually unquestioned, extending the command to honor mothers is breathtaking. Here, God acknowledges women as instruments of God's creative power on a par with men and worthy of the same reverence. Life is sacred and all who play a role in bringing us to life are to be revered.

To honor parents is not fundamentally about the parents themselves. It is not even about family, at least not in the way that we understand family today in much of North American society. Families, while often loving and generous, were more than mere affiliation or affection groups in the ancient world. They were economic unions. Family mergers in the form of marriage were carefully crafted with an eye on the long-term benefits to both families involved. Families depended on each member fulfilling specific roles. If all pulled together they could survive and thrive. If not, disaster was often the result. Honoring parents was about survival.

Problems arose when parents got old and could no longer work to help support the family. When this happened, they could become an economic drain that threatened the whole family. It was not unknown for families to abandon older parents who could no longer contribute. These old people had little choice but to beg or to die. In a culture that, at least in principle, honored elders and the wisdom that they brought to a community, this abandonment was seen as shameful. Sometimes families became so desperate to find a way to deal with their elderly parents that they brought them to Jerusalem for the great festivals and left them there. By the time of the early church movement in the years after Jesus' resurrection, a startling number of families left their vulnerable elderly for the impoverished Jerusalem church to deal with. These decisions were not made out of meanness. They were made out of perceived necessity.

Honoring the Life Givers

In our day, those painful decisions are still with us. In the early days of the coronavirus pandemic, when the brunt of the virus' first wave disproportionately affected the elderly or otherwise infirm, the belief that these people are spent anyway and should just go ahead and die so we can get back to economic normalcy was not subtle. Sometimes still, desperation, or skewed values, lead people to accept circumstances and ethical choices that would otherwise be unthinkable.

To hear the call to honor parents is a reminder from God that it is not productivity that gives value. Life is the ultimate gift that God gives to the human family. It is to be given its due weight at every stage. To honor parents is to honor those whom God uses to bring us to life. Lineage is at the heart of the promise given to Abraham and Sarah as our family story began. The text of the Fifth Word tells us that to honor the life givers will in return give us long life in the land of promised blessing. In other words, the promise itself rests on how we honor life and those who are its vehicles.

For those of us who grew up in families with loving and honorable parents, this Word may not present much of a challenge. I grew up in such a family. My parents were never harsh. Nor were they pushovers. They made contributions to the community and taught me right from wrong. They were not perfect people. They had wounds of their own, as we all do. Still, they were people that almost anyone would consider worthy of respect and honor.

In families like that, some of us may have the tendency to give too much weight to our parents' thoughts, opinions, and needs, and, as a result, become slow to find our own voices and priorities. This can be a way of dishonoring as well. Finding the line between being absorbed by the needs and values of our parents and being nourished by them to become who we really are, is in many ways the high calling of honoring.

While separating and becoming our true selves can be difficult for some of us who came from nurturing families, it can be even more fraught for those who want to do nothing more than flee their families. For good or ill, we take our families with us no matter how far and long we run.

Early in my study of this Word, I wrote to a colleague who I knew had grown up in awful circumstances. His parents were, charitably, less than honorable. His father abandoned the family and his mother was cruel. He once told the story of when he was a little boy, after his father left, he and his mother were shopping in town. He saw his father across the street and called to him. The father turned, looked at his son, gave no acknowledgment and walked away. He told that story at age fifty, and the pain was still palpable.

I knew that despite all of that, my friend took care of both of his parents when they were aged. I asked him how he dealt with this Word in light of his experiences. He wrote back a thoughtful and touching response. For him, honoring his parents was a duty that was based not on love of them, but on love of Christ. He said that he chose to visit them regularly to make sure that they did not fall into circumstances that are degrading to any human being. He did that so that no matter what happened, past or present, there could be something of the dignity that is due to all life, the most precious gift of God. He said, "If I were not a Christian, I am sure that I would have nothing to do with them. But I am, and I honor them so that I do not neglect my roots and because they are the instruments through which God gave me this life that I can live with Christ." Wow.

At a stewardship retreat once, I noticed a middle-aged woman hanging toward the back of the sanctuary where we were meeting. She was lovely, with big soft eyes and curly salt-and-pepper hair. She didn't share in the group discussion, but when we took our break she came up to me shyly.

Never making full eye contact, she told me that she had grown up in a home where her parents drank too much and had little left to give her in the way of attention or faith formation. Each Sunday, as a young child, however, her grandfather came to the family home and took the little girl to worship. He was a very strict old school Presbyterian. It being the Sabbath, he would not drive his car. He saw that as work. So they walked together to the little church a few blocks away. Each Sunday, she dressed herself in her best dress, put on her matching socks and wiped her little shoes until they shone. She and her grandfather walked solemnly, her hands folded in front of her and her steps halting, like a bride.

She loved the church with the twangy piano and the old organ that shook the floor. She loved Sunday school and making pictures of Jesus with the one lost lamb on his shoulders. She even sat through worship most weeks without complaint, ears pricked for words or stories that she knew.

One Sunday, when she was about six years old, she was especially excited because she had a new dress with a puffy petticoat and little raised violets on the skirt. All went as usual until toward the end of the service. It was a Communion Sunday and the elements were being passed on metal trays in the pews. When the tray with the bread was handed to her, she mistook it for the offering plate and dropped her dime into the plate with a clang.

Her grandfather was outraged. He grabbed her by the arm and took her, confused and crying, down the center aisle and out of the church. It had rained the night before and he made her sit in her new dress in a mud puddle until the service ended. Then she stood in her muddy finery and through her tears had to apologize to every worshiper as each exited.

As she told me this story I am sure that my shock registered on my face. I had no idea what to say. She then went on to tell me that she had not thought of this experience in many years. When I asked the group to try to recall their earliest memory of money and to think what they had learned in that experience, it all came flooding back to her. "I realized," she said, "why I have never felt comfortable coming into the front door of a church. I always come in the side. I never felt worthy again." Old sins cast long shadows. So do parental, or in this case grandparental, wounds.

Our families of origin are not perfect. Neither are we as parents. Sometimes the imperfections are easily soothed by a kiss and an apology. Sometimes they are not. Sometimes human parents fail utterly. Sometimes their own brokenness leaves them crippled in their parenting. Sometimes they fail, thinking they are doing the right thing. Sometimes they fail because they are powerless in situations that are bigger than they are. Sometimes parents get confused and overwhelmed and have favorites and feel helpless. Sometimes, despite their best efforts, nothing they do seems to come out right. Sometimes parents leave. Sometimes parents die, leaving behind gaping wounds that decades of life can't fill or heal. Stepparenting is a gift and a challenge as well. If the separations are not fully healed, the new family configurations can be filled with stress and resentments.

The insidious thing about painful parenting, whether that is birth parents, adoptive parents, stepparents, grandparents, or foster parents, is that it can set in motion dynamics that go on for many generations. Patterns of pain are learned early and often broken late. However, they can be broken. Old tapes can be recorded over.

Healing the Wounds of Painful Parenting

The Scriptures themselves witness to the power of God to make up for and redeem human failings. Our biblical ancestors are esteemed, but they are also not perfect, nor do they parent perfectly. In Genesis 21, when Sarah is overcome with jealousy at the sight of Abraham's first-born son Ishmael, born to the enslaved Hagar, she insists that Abraham expel the son from the household and his mother with him. It is her son, Isaac, that she is convinced should take priority. The family lives with the consequences of that rupture to this day. The children of Isaac, the Jewish people, and the children of Ishmael, the Islamic people, have not yet been able to fully heal the multigenerational wound between them.

This story, by any standard I can conceive, is one of parenting gone terribly wrong. The glimmer of blessing we find in it is that, even in all of its messiness and pain, God intervenes to save and provide blessing for Hagar and Ishmael as well as Isaac.

When human parents fail miserably, our heavenly parent will not fail. God searches and finds a way when there seems to be no way at all. God will be our parent even if we have no others.

How does God parent us? God does this in ways that are unique to our individual and community needs. If we are lost and need guidance, God may bring a passage of Scripture to mind or put a book in our hands at just the right moment. If we have sinned terribly, God will help us learn from our mistakes and provide new opportunities to do better, even if we have foreclosed on all the ones we saw. If our communities have descended into rampant injustice, God will cheer us on and give us energy to continue our work. If our parents or families fail us, God will find others to help.

Often God re-parents us through our lives of prayer. Sometimes our times of prayer are sporadic and seem to be little more than a list of our desires. Like children sitting in Santa's lap, after standing in line for hours, we pour out the laundry list of things or outcomes that, if God could just manage it for us, life would be great. I suspect we've all been there. These are not bad prayers. They may not be mature prayers, but we are not always mature. Sometimes we just need to take our wants to God in the hope that somehow that transaction will release the storehouses of heaven or at least change the way we look at things. God welcomes us when we are small, and our wishes not well thought out. God listens and ultimately does what is best for all involved.

God parents us, too, in subtle ways, when our prayer deepens, and we open the eyes of our hearts to bigger things. Like teenagers awakening to the world and its needs, we come to God with our desire for change in the world around us. We ask for a mission and courage to undertake it. We ask for a partner with whom to share our lives. We ask for rewards and blessing from doing right. God receives these prayers with tender understanding of what we really need and what our role in the drama of life will turn out to be. In this prayer, God parents us by sorting, pointing, and picking us up when we fall on our faces and skin our fragile egos.

God parents us as we get older and prayer shifts from listing our wants and needs to lifting up the needs of those we love. In this prayer, God parents us by opening our hearts more and more and caring tenderly for the heartbreak that naturally follows an increase in loving. In this prayer, we sometimes just sit with God and lift up the ones we love without words, imagine them as vessels waiting to be filled with love, healing, courage, or insight. God welcomes these prayers and parents us by planting an ever-renewing supply of empathy and a sense of belonging to a family much larger than our own.

God parents us in prayer that is none of those things as well. God shapes us with the traditional prayers of our liturgies. God shapes us when we release all words and sit, waiting to receive a sense of presence. Like grown children sitting quietly on the porch with a grandparent, we wait. Sometimes a flood of stories comes. Sometimes we just sip tea together. In these prayers, God opens to us who we really are, enjoys our presence, and strengthens our sense of belonging to God and all that God is bringing forth in the world.

God also parents us through the church. Throughout its history we have called the gathering of the faithful, Mother Church. In the church, we are raised up in the things of God, molded and encouraged. In church, wisdom is shared and pondered, sacraments are offered and do their mighty work in us. John Calvin, the Swiss reformer of the sixteenth century, who is a patriarch of the Reformed churches, called the church Mother and the Eucharist the Mother's Milk of the faithful.

The church has been no more perfect a parent than any other, however. As church, sometimes we have been slow to welcome change, quick to find fault, too sure our way is the only way. In those times, we have wounded our children and they have fled us, just as a child might flee an abusive home at the first opportunity. Still, God reforms and is always reforming the church, continually working to make the community of faith look more like the body of Christ into which we have been made. Like children who leave home hurt, sometimes we, too, come back to the church and find that reconciliation is possible because we have all changed.

Ending the Cycle of Pain

Over the years, as I have pondered this Word, and thought about the fallout of parental failures, I have wondered how the cycle of painful parenting can end. John Calvin dealt with the problem by simply releasing children from the obligation of this Word if their parents were not due honoring. I'm not so sure about that. Perhaps honoring has to take many shapes.

Eighty percent of the pastoral counseling hours I've spent over the last thirty-plus years have in one way or another dealt with family pain. Probably more than that. I have come to believe that one of the most profound ways that we honor problematic parents is by choosing to do whatever we must to stop the cycle of pain. We decide that it will end with us.

We honor the life our parents gave us by choosing to be released from the bondage that came with it. If alcohol ravaged three generations, we can choose to stop it in the fourth. If criticism was a way of life, we can choose to stop the pattern. If rigidity and anger marred our childhoods, we can practice openness and gratitude. The list goes on and on. These statements are simple. The work is not. It is, however, profoundly honoring of our parents when we stop the pain with us and choose to nurture the life in ourselves that they could not.

The work of stopping the cycles of pain in a family system or community requires honesty about the damage done and willingness to forgive and release the one who has hurt us. To forgive is never to excuse, or to say that what happened was somehow okay. By definition, it was not okay, or forgiveness would not be necessary.

Forgiveness is a choice we make when we decide we have hurt long enough. It is a choice we make when we decide that what has happened to us has taken up enough space in our lives and does not get to rule us any longer. We do not have to wait to feel forgiving in order to forgive. Neither does forgiveness require contrition or recompense from the one who hurt us. It is not really about them at all. It is about our freedom from the wounds inflicted. It is about our decision that what has happened to us in the past does not get to define the future.

Forgiveness can be healing when done in person. That is not always possible or prudent, however. Forgiveness can also be healing when done in our hearts in prayer or with another trusted and safe person. All that is needed is to tell the story honestly and choose to release the other person. In so doing we claim our own release. Life rushes into the spaces freed up by the release of stored up wounds and the pain of carrying unforgiveness.[1]

In thinking about the Fifth Word, for some of us, the forgiveness that we need to offer is to ourselves. Perhaps we feel guilt that we did not do enough. We may feel that our lives got so busy that we neglected parents' needs as they aged. We may feel guilty that we missed out on moments we could have shared, small kindnesses we could have offered because we were so wrapped up in our responsibilities or lives. On a deeper level, we may feel guilty that we were not able to somehow fix the hurts of our parents. They bandaged our knees, but we could not mend the holes in their hearts from their own journeys and losses. This can be especially true if a parent is widowed or divorced or lost their own parents young. In these cases, it is not forgiveness that is called for, since no wrong has been committed. We are not responsible for doing what is not ours to do. Here we must offer ourselves a measure of grace and remember that God will do what we cannot. Releasing the false responsibility to do for parents what we ultimately cannot do, is a powerful way of honoring them. It assumes that they are fully whole human beings on a sacred journey that we accompany but do not control. Releasing in this way has the added benefit of creating space inside of us to see our parents as autonomous and not merely extensions of ourselves. Then we are able to love and honor with new depth and trust.

It Takes a "Crash"

Life is much more than biology. It is infused with Being itself and mirrors God's own nature and character. Life is the primary gift and at the heart everything in the theology of the Old Testament.

God, in this Word, asks us to honor those whom God uses to bring us to the fullness of life and not only those who bring us biological life. Sometimes the life givers in our lives are not our parents. When we realize our parents' limitations, recognize that they gave us what they had to give, and find peace with that, then God encourages us to broaden our gaze and see other life givers and our need for them.

Several years ago, Robbie and I visited the San Diego Zoo Safari Park in California. We took a cart safari that allowed us a close-up look at some of the animals in their wide-open habitats. We rounded a curve in the trail and there, bunched up together under a sturdy shade tree, sat about six female rhinoceroses. Our guide told us that they were part of a conservation project to help save the species. For years, rhinos steadfastly refused to breed in captivity. Every possible enticement was used to encourage it, but none of the healthy breeding pairs produced. Finally, by happenstance, they learned that female rhinos, when deprived of the company of other females, will suppress their hormones so as not to conceive.

They do this because in the wild they need to have several adult females to protect a calf from predators. Why go through an eighteen-month gestation just to have the little guy gotten by a lion while a baby? Without a "sisterhood" they would have none of it. When several females bonded into a group, called a crash (don't you love that?), then they felt safe to conceive, brought their hormones up to speed and had at it. More than fifty of the endangered babies have been born this way.

That day in San Diego, we rounded that bend and there they were, a crash of rhino sisters under a tree in the summer sun, each taking a turn looking after the one young calf. Huge, funny-looking things with 800-pound heads, under a shade tree taking turns babysitting. It takes a crash—whether it's our family or our chosen family, our friends—to bring life to life.

In those days of isolation and distancing during the pandemic, I became more and more aware of how much my crash brings me to life day in and day out, year in and year out. I began to learn this in the spring of 1976. I was in my last semester of college when I fell very ill. For reasons unknown, I am prone to blood clots. That spring, the clots formed and threw to my lungs. I was in critical condition.

At one point, my doctor, a young resident who happened to be a Presbyterian elder, came into my darkened room. He sat down beside me and drew a picture on the back of his prescription pad of what was happening in my lungs. He illuminated it with one of those little penlights that doctors use to look up a person's nose. He told me there was nothing else they knew to do and, given that, he did not know if I would survive the night.

Outside, my roommate Susan, several friends from my sorority, some of the guys from Chi Phi fraternity, where I was a Little Sister, my hometown friends Laura and Harriett, and others sat in the waiting room. There they sat, scared, young as morning, surrounded by chip bags and unopened textbooks, waiting. My crash.

They came in to visit, one by one. Susan came in first. She brought me lipstick and brushed my hair. I could hear her struggling not to cry as the brush pulled through my wild, red Farrah Fawcett hair. I learned later that she postponed the comprehensive exams for her master's degree to be there with me that night and to take care of my mother for the three weeks I was in the hospital.

I remember my friend Belinda coming in and Harriett who has been there for me for everything since third grade. Several of the guys, sheepish, unused to fearing death, came shuffling in with carnations and funny get-well cards and invitations to dances if I would just get well.

Last came my friend Laura, who was present at my first birthday party. She was doing her student teaching that semester. She came in with a huge straw bag/purse, sat down on the foot of my bed and began to tell stories of her classroom. It didn't take long before I noticed that her purse was moving. Not only that, it was quacking! "What in heavens name?" I said.

At that moment, a little wild-eyed duckling sprang from her purse and began to run around on my bed, quacking, pecking at tubes, and tunneling beneath covers. We laughed until nurses came and sternly told Laura that wild animals were prohibited in the hospital. We laughed some more. Then we cried and she left.

After the visitors were back in the waiting room or gone home to their dorms, Dr. Keller came back. He sat next to me all that night and read from his pocket New Testament and Psalms. He held the little green book in one hand and the penlight in the other, page after page, lament and faith. *Yea though I walk through the valley of the shadow . . . How long, O Lord . . . Bless the Lord, O my soul.* When dawn began to break, he left to wash up for his rounds. Still then we did not know if the crisis had passed, but I will never forget what he said to me as he put his penlight and Bible in the pocket of his lab coat. "Miss Gamble," he said. "It has been a privilege."

As I look back on that night, I realize it's possible I have conflated several nights into one. What I know is, that young elder and my dear friends—each one of them was Christ for me. Even the duckling! That night, my crash labored to bring me to life again.

Sometimes the life givers we are asked to honor are not just those who literally birthed or raised us, but also all of those ones that see us through. We give due place to those who have taught us things we needed to know, how to tie our shoes, or how to apply mascara, how to study for a test, or how to keep going when our heart is breaking. God invites us to give a place of priority in our lives to those who build us up, raise us up, hold us up. God asks us to give the life bearers a place of honor.

The survival of the beloved community depends on our recognizing that we cannot go it alone. We need the wisdom, power, and protection of the community in order to survive. In the very heart of the Scriptures lies the truth that without community, without others to share the load, without a tribe to call ones' own, without those who know all, see all, and accept all, the tender young shoots of our lives would be too vulnerable to survive. Without the life bearers, everything we are created to bring forth is stopped in its tracks. It is a blessing when our families play that role. Still, even when they can and do, that is too much freight for a few to carry. It is crucial for our well-being and for future generations that we find and honor those who bring us to life and who bear up our lives.

Honoring the Legacies of Our Life Givers

Honoring the life givers does not stop with their earthly lives. It is possible to honor parents and other life givers after they have died. We do that by telling their stories. The rabbis taught that no one was ever really dead while someone was left who remembers them. We are the promise that our parents planted. We are their future.

When we tell our parents' stories, we re-member, give flesh again, to their lives. We honor the humanity in them with all of its nuances. If I share with you the story of my father as a young district attorney during the height of the civil rights movement in Alabama and tell you that he valiantly tried the murder case of Viola Liuzzo, the mother who came to Selma to march to Montgomery and was killed by Klansmen, I honor him by introducing you to his public life. When I share that he lost the case with a hung jury, ten to convict her murderer and two to acquit, all male and all white, but he never felt the moral victory that others saw and built upon, I show a bit more of him. But when I tell you that my first memory of him is sitting on the back porch listening to an Alabama football game on the radio and him wrapping my fingers around a red and white shaker, or tell you how he taught me to dance the fox trot by putting my feet on his and dancing me around the living room, or how every time I left home he stood on the porch and waved until my car was out of sight, I honor not just the life he led, but the life he instilled in me. Even if we only tell the stories in our memories or to God in prayer, we keep the promise alive.

If our stories are not sweet, when we tell them, we still heal bit by bit and honor the vast resiliency of life itself. If those who hurt us are long gone and took our hopes for a different outcome with them, we can still heal by telling the story. To do so doesn't excuse our parents or whitewash our experience. It sanctifies it and gives us the power to shape the lives we want to leave to our children and grandchildren.

The Fifth Word asks that we honor our life givers, give them due priority and tell their stories. It also asks us to live honorably so that those who come after us will have worthy stories to tell and to continue. The Fifth Word asks that we shape our lives to be daily life givers. The call to give honor is a simultaneous call to be honorable and to parent well as we are able even if, like me, we do not have birth children of our own.

On my last day of service as pastor of First Presbyterian Church in Birmingham, Alabama, the congregation hosted a celebration and farewell lunch for me. It was beautiful, kind, and hard. There was a long line of people who stood for an hour or more for one more hug and to say a word to me.

At one point, I noticed a little five-year-old boy in the congregation. He faithfully stood in the line even after his mother encouraged him to come and have an ice cream or to let her take him home. He would have none of it. When he finally got to me, his eyes were brimming with tears. "Are you having fun?" he asked. Before I could answer he said, "I'm not having all that much fun. I hate this," he said. "Me too," I said. At which point, we both sat down on the floor and held each other and cried.

After a while, as he walked away, he turned back and said, "I will never forget you." No doubt he now has, but in the moment, I was powerfully honored. My associate pastor came up to me after the line had died down and said, "Eugenia, you have been mother to many." Like all mothers, sometimes I've done that well and sometimes poorly indeed. The point is, that we, no matter our circumstances, have the honor of parenting the future. It is an honor with which God entrusts us. To do that well, we look back and find gratitude and peace and we look forward and see hope.

Conclusion

Each of the Ten Words carries within it a call that is deeper than the injunctions. In this Word, we are called both to honor those who bring us to life and to be honorable life givers ourselves. We each, whether we are parents or not, have the opportunity to honorably parent future generations by the choices that we make and the lives we live.

The wound that this Word seeks to heal is the pain of disconnection, of feeling that we are somehow not rooted to the human family and a particular people. God desires nothing more than that we have a place and a people. That is at the heart of promise itself. Honoring that place and those people releases loneliness and replaces it, over time, with identity and contentment. This Word calls us to honor life. The Sixth Word takes us further, asking us to consider whether or not honoring life ever has its limits.

Spiritual Practice: Praying for the Life Givers

Pause and think about the life givers in your life. Think of your parents and thank them for the gift of life that God used them to bring to you. Think about the ancestors and the wisdom that has been life-giving for generations. Think about all of those who have taught you, bandaged you up, cheered you on, forgiven you, and believed in you. Thank God for each one. If possible, reach out to them with a note, card, or call. Make a commitment to be a life giver in your family, community, and world. You will be used in large or small ways to heal.

Take a moment to write a prayer for your parents. Thank God for what they gave you. If you are ready, forgive them for any lingering wounds. If you never knew them, introduce yourself. Then spend some time praying for all mothers and fathers everywhere, especially for those who are struggling to provide for their families or who have lost children. Parenting is hard. All parents need our support and honoring.

Questions for Personal and Group Reflection

1. Who have been the most important life givers in your life?
2. What qualities of your parents do you admire? What qualities do you want to release?
3. How do you experience God as parent? The church as parent?
4. What commitments to parenting future generations do you feel called to make?
5. Who are the parents in your community who seem to be most in need? How can you honor them? What about global parents? What about Mother Church and Mother Earth? How can you honor them?

CHAPTER 6

MURDER MOST FOUL

*Addressing the Tendency to Violence,
Anger, and Cruelty*

You shall not murder.
—Exodus 20:13

I remember the day vividly. It was springtime, April. I was making my way up the coast of Oregon on my way to Portland after speaking at a mission conference in Eugene. Rather than take the freeway straight north, my then-husband and I decided that we wanted to see the rocky, wild Oregon coast. So we set off west until the ragged Pacific mountain range fell away and we had to either turn north or swim.

The drive from Eugene to the coast was beautiful, meadows and woodlands filled with elk and rhododendron and as green as the east. These were the days before cell phones and GPS. I had a map and the sweet anonymity of a strange road. It was a crystal-clear day, no clouds anywhere, just the expanse of sea and the mystic wonder of recognizing one's own smallness against the vastness of sea and sky.

Farther up the road, right at the town where we would turn back inland to make our way to Portland, we stopped for an early dinner at an ocean-front café, that, unexpectedly, was managed by a man from Dauphin Island, Alabama, the little spot on the map that is now my home.

The young waiter came up to me and asked how I was. "I'm fine," I said. "How are you?"

He paused for a long moment, not looking at me, looking instead in an unseeing way, at the order pad he held in his hand. "I'm pensive, I think," he said.

Instantly, I was on alert. The "pastor on duty" sign in my head clicked neon. "Is something the matter?" I asked.

"Oh," he said. "You haven't heard."

"Heard what?" I asked, feeling a growing alarm.

"I'm not going to tell you," he responded, almost backing away from me.

"Oh yes, you are!" I said, mustering every bit of motherly or pastoral authority I could find.

"Well," he said, "there has been a shooting. In a high school. In Denver."

I gulped. "What?"

"Yes," he said. "A bunch of kids are dead."

"What high school? I lived in Denver. I lived in a suburb called Littleton."

"It was a flower I think," he said.

"Columbine," I whispered. "That's in Littleton."

"That's it," he said. "What can I get you?"

"I can't think," I said.

"How about I bring you a bowl of soup or something?"

"Perfect," I said.

When he left, I remember staring at the water in total shock and horror.

I tried to remember which of the kids in my youth group were still at that high school.

I closed my eyes, hoping somehow that when I opened them, time would have rolled back and none of it would be true.

But it was true. Thirteen kids shot in their high school by two of their classmates who then turned their guns on themselves. Thirteen kids gunned down in their school. Now Columbine no longer even lists in the top ten deadliest shootings in recent years in our country.

The Sixth Word is one of the most complex and beautiful of the Ten. This Word is about how human beings are to (or not to) handle our fear, helplessness, and the rage that grows out of them. Up until this point, each of the Words has come with an explanation or a promise attached. When we arrive at the Sixth Word, all of that evaporates, almost seems quaint. Here, in the Hebrew text, we have only two words: no murder. There is not a "thou shalt not" exactly. Just a strongly made statement of fact. In the beloved community, we do not kill each other.

Much of the scholarship and controversy that have swirled around this Word for millennia centers on the Hebrew root word *rahtz-akh*. It is not the word most often used in the Old Testament for "to kill." Does this word refer, then, only to intentional murder with malice? Or does it, more broadly, refer to killing in general? A careful look at the other places in the Old Testament where this word is used (Deut. 4:41–42, Num. 35:20–21 and 35:30, for example) shows a range of meanings. Biblical scholar Terence E. Fretheim, in his *Exodus* commentary, concludes that the Sixth Word must be understood broadly. He says that the Word prohibits "any act of violence against an individual out of hatred, anger, malice, deceit or for personal gain, in whatever circumstance, by whatever method that might result in death, even if unintentional."[1]

It is easy to see how the Sixth Word is a companion and extension of the Fifth. Honor the life givers. Don't be a life taker. Once again, life itself is the value. Life is God's gift and death is the enemy.

Life and Death

We cannot discuss the Sixth Word without coming to terms with death itself. To do so we must acknowledge from the start that we are dealing in the realm of mystery. It is an enigma that inspires human emotions of such intensity that we cover our uncertainty and discomfort with an amazing array of euphemisms designed to soften or distance us from the reality and its implications. "Perish. Expire. Passed. Croaked. Kicked the bucket. Bought the farm. Taking a dirt bath."

No matter how hard we try to domesticate death or soften the blow, it releases in us the most powerful human emotions of hostility, anguish, relief, longing, great love, and deep hate.

They burst forth as if from nowhere no matter how prepared we think we are.

While doing my clinical chaplaincy training, I had to tell a young man that his father had died after a particularly risky surgery. The doctor explained carefully what had happened, and, as was the policy of the hospital, I told the man his father had died. He listened carefully and attentively to the doctor, but when I said that his father had died, he picked up a big metal trash can and threw it at me, knocking me to the floor, and cutting my leg.

When I stumbled up from the floor, with the doctor dabbing at my bleeding leg with tissues, the young man threw his arms around me, wept bitterly, and asked me if I would do his father's funeral, which he hoped would focus on his release from suffering and reunion with his beloved wife who had died two years before.

Death provides a crucible for human passion made even more profound by our inability to explain the why of it, control and contain the how and when of it, or comprehend the "what comes next" of it.

The Scriptures themselves do not provide us with a unified and orderly theology of death. In the incredibly rich fabric of the Hebrew Scriptures, death is inextricably woven together with life from beginning to end. There is never any attempt to deny the power of death nor to sanitize emotions surrounding it. Israel understood physical death as the natural resolution of physical life. It was a given. When a person lived a righteous life, died in advanced years with many descendants, death was mourned ritually and then accepted as a natural God-given reality, and therefore somehow in our best interest.

The predominant emotion expressed with regard to early death in the Old Testament is not fear. Rather, the feelings are of anger and hostility for its radical challenge to a life of praise. Even in the deep emotions surrounding death there is, in Israel's radical monotheism, an unassailable belief that life and death belong to God. It is only as a result of God's will that we live. It is only as a result of God's will that we die.

In the New Testament, the view changes. Death itself, while not sought, is welcomed as the ultimate glory and entrée into the heavenly realm. Death is never viewed, in the New Testament, apart from the lens of resurrection hope. Through that lens, death is defeated as a power to thwart life or to end being. Death becomes, at best, a reunion with the Lord (Col. 5:8) and ultimate gain (Phil. 1:24) and, at worst, irrelevant, as in the Gospel of John in which eternal life begins at the moment of a believer's surrender to God. On the other side of the resurrection, death has no ultimate power for the believer because praise can never be stopped, and good-byes are never final.

Life and Death Belong to God

As different and nuanced as both the Old Testament and New Testament views are, they have one thing in common. Life and death are in God's hands alone. With that view, it is entirely outside the prerogative of human beings to kill each other. It is an assault on God and an affront to creation itself. The ancient rabbis called killing "armed robbery of God." Still, we kill, and we always have.

Rattle Fatigue

Shortly before the 9/11 attack, a periodical came across my desk that contained a startling article about a medical/psychological condition being documented in children in the Middle East, called Rattle Fatigue.[2] Rattle Fatigue is what happens to people when they are in a situation in which they are chronically threatened or feel unsafe. When a person is in a situation of violence, surprise, insecurity, in which the accepted rules for how life is to work do not apply anymore, the person who suffers from Rattle Fatigue begins to numb out. It is simply too exhausting to feel what would be normal to feel. What should not have happened has happened, and it wasn't a onetime thing. Because of that, sufferers become hyper alert and deadened at the same time. Anything can happen and it does, so, oh well.

For many of us, a kind of Rattle Fatigue set in after 9/11. It has increased and been reinforced with every mass shooting or unfathomable tragedy since. For some of us, Rattle Fatigue has been a way of life as long as we can remember. If we grew up in a violent home, if we lived in neighborhoods marred by systemic inequities and generational poverty, we may never have felt safe to respond with a full range of emotions to our life situations. In Rattle Fatigue, the spectrum of emotions is distilled to two—numbness or fury—and the swing between the two can happen in the blink of an eye. I know this personally.

In 1975, the August before my senior year in college, my father, a state judge, was the victim of an assassination attempt with a car bomb in our side yard. I was home from summer school and was to be heading back to university that day. I remember leaping from my bed at the sound of the blast. My mother, who was also in the car but unharmed physically, yelled for me to call an ambulance. She thought he had been shot. I stopped in my tracks, numbly called for an ambulance, called the police, and got towels for tourniquets. When the nurses and ER doctors ran down the street with a stretcher from the local hospital a block away, I calmly picked up my father's calf muscle from the driveway and put it on the stretcher as they wheeled him away to surgery. I remember feeling a ghostly calm, a vacancy of the heart. Mercifully he survived, in many ways less traumatized than the rest of us.

Weeks later, when I went back to school, Alabama Bureau of Investigation agents had examined my car with a fine-toothed comb and left it for me in my parking space at the Student Union. I remember getting into it and trying to get up the nerve to put the key in the ignition. I shook so hard I had to get someone to help me. Since that time, every time I hear an explosion on TV or even a car backfire in the street, I taste gun powder in my mouth. Violence kills more than the body. It can kill confidence, a sense of safety and place in the world. It can leave us wondering if life has value at all. That is Rattle Fatigue.

Kill Energy

Violence and murder release a kind of kill energy that multiplies, becomes increasingly deadly and, as it does so, becomes increasingly more mundane, until the lives involved seem like they are not lives at all. The sacredness of each human being dims. Love contracts. We are no longer family. It is us versus them. Anything goes.

One of the unsettling things about the Sixth Word is that we are to be held accountable not just for what we do, but also by our complicity in what others do. Or even what we, or others, fail to do. *Rahtz-akh* happens actively and passively.

After the Columbine massacre, the pastor of the Lutheran church where one of the shooters had been an active member of the youth group preached the boy's funeral to a near-empty sanctuary. He used the text from 2 Samuel 18 in which we find the decisive battle of the civil war instigated by King David's son, Absalom, against his father. When the messenger arrives to tell David that the battle is won and he is restored to the throne, he asks about his son and is told that he has been killed. In one of the most poignant passages in the Bible, David climbs his chamber steps, broken of heart, saying, "O my son Absalom, my son, my son Absalom! Would that I had died instead of you, O Absalom, my son, my son!" (2 Sam. 18:33)

In preaching the young shooter's funeral, the pastor read this text and substituted the boy's name for that of Absalom. "O my son, Dylan, my son, my son Dylan! Would that I had died instead of you, O Dylan, my son, my son." In that moment, he reminded all of us that, just as David's choices played a role in who his son became, we too make choices and bear some culpability for the violence that surges around and through us.

Granted, most of us have not killed anyone, although some may have in an accident or war or some other situation. Most of our ancient ancestors did not kill each other either. Still, this Word is not one that we can skip over lightly and think it does not apply to us. We play a role in the violence and cruelty of our times either by what we do or what we do not do every day. We do it even by what we see and what we refuse to see.

There is even a kill energy that we can find creeping into our language and norms. Kill pain. Kill cancer cells. Kill viruses. Kill thoughts. Kill murderers. Kill enemies. Kill anyone that momentarily threatens us. The problem is that using kill energy as a means to right wrongs, restore some semblance of equilibrium or safety, will never do what we intend. It will just add to the sum total of pain in the world. In this Word, God reminds us that killing will never restore balance.

Jesus returns to this truth in his astonishingly radical Sermon on the Mount in which he tells those who follow him that we are to counter kill energy with prayer, examination of our hearts, and a radical change of mindset. He points out that even anger is a form of murder and subject to judgment (Matt. 5:22). Jesus recognizes that every action begins with a thought. When we nurse anger it produces kill energy and kill energy will always find an outlet. Anyone or anything can be too easily sacrificed to our anger and need to return to emotional equilibrium. Just as creation begins with a word, murder begins with a thought.

Jesus goes on to tell us that the way we are to treat enemies is to love and pray for them. He reminds us that in the new realm of God, there is no retaliation, no revenge, no annihilation of enemies. In the realm of God, we only work for the highest good of all. Anger healed. Cheeks turned. Enemies prayed for. God left to sort it all out. (Matt. 5:38–48).

In the early days of Christianity, disobeying this Word was seen as a crime against both creation and incarnation. To kill is to diminish the divine expression itself as all are created in the image of God. To kill is to thwart how God is seeking to be made known and visible in the world. Each human life reflects a bit of divine life, even if that glimmer is faint to our sight because of hurt, sin, rebellion, or prejudice.

There is much about this Word that is beyond the scope of this book and my ability. How do we decide when a human life begins or ends? The ancients thought that life was in the breath. God breathed it into us, and life began. Is that good enough for us now? In the intensive care unit, do we take over God's prerogative by using a ventilator to keep breath flowing? Is it ever appropriate to take a life by euthanasia or the death penalty? Is war forbidden by this Word? What about self-defense? What about militarized policing?

The particulars of our wrestling with contemporary issues are different in many ways from those of our biblical ancestors who assigned the death penalty for disobedient children and launched innumerable wars because they thought God told them to do so. The issues are also, in many ways, the same. Does the preserving of life have limits? Is anyone irredeemable? Does anyone deserve death? Is hastening death ever a moral good? Each of us must wrestle with those questions and find our place to stand. Clearly, we will not all find the same place to stand.

Sources of Kill Energy

Perhaps before we can find our places to stand, it might be helpful to think about the roots of the kill energy that erupts in violence around us nearly daily. One source of kill energy is toxic rage. By toxic rage, I mean out-of-control anger, either undirected, misdirected, or even appropriately directed, that occurs as a result of real or perceived wounds or threats. Rage seeks to hurt or destroy in order to restore a sense of power, control, protection, equilibrium, and, in some sense, fairness.[3] It is this kind of rage that bubbles up into mass shootings all the while feeling righteous and necessary to the killers.

The Sixth Word reminds us that we cannot kill away our problems. We cannot kill away our fears. We cannot kill away our enemies or those that we find abhorrent. Killing something or someone does not reconcile accounts. It can't. Only light and love can do that. Only God can do that, so, only God has authority over life and death. When we kill, even when we just rely on toxic rage to face our challenges, we choose death over life and take from God that which we do not have the power to restore.

In addition to unfettered rage, unreconciled or toxic shame fuels kill energy and the culture it creates. By shame, I don't mean healthy feelings of guilt when we are ashamed of having done something that we should be ashamed of having done. Toxic shame doesn't have to do with feelings about what we have done. Rather, it has to do with our feelings about who we are.

Toxic shame is the feeling that something is wrong with us, that we are bad, not because of what we do, but because of our very nature. Toxic shame often includes feeling that we are powerless to face the situations of our lives because we are chronically defective. This kind of internal lie can leave us feeling that the security, love, and respect that we want is forever outside our reach and that we secretly deserve it to be that way. If we don't know ourselves well, if we do not know our beloved status with God, if we do not have the spiritual or emotional tools or support to examine our situations, then shame often gets misplaced and comes out in destruction or self-destruction. "It was my fault," the battered spouse says to the doctor who sets her broken arm. "I didn't want to do it. They made me do it. It had to be done," says one killer after another.

Another related issue that causes violence and murder to become normalized and even lauded, is toxic individualism.[4] The sense that "I can do it myself and nobody can stop me" is in some ways baked into United States dominant culture. It is a story line that runs through our sense of ourselves and buoys our views of our heroes. It teaches us that there are really no barriers to our getting what we want and believe we deserve. Individual character is the only thing that determines success or failure.

When this story line is firmly entrenched in us and we still experience threat or failure, we often lash out. It is somebody else's fault. It has to be. Nothing else fits the story we have adopted in our minds to understand our lives. This kind of threatened story line allows people to begin to see others as not real people and therefore it doesn't matter what we do to them. It becomes a feeder for rampant racism, as we saw in the early genocidal days of our country's founding and as we saw when enslaved people were considered three-fifths human. When this becomes an accepted story line, protesters easily become thugs and deserving of death or anything we do to them. This mindset leads to things like the mayor of a small Alabama town resigning under pressure saying, after an angry rant about Black Lives Matter and homosexuals, "The only way to change it would be to kill the problem out."[5]

Kill energy fueled by out-of-control individualism can be seen when people refuse to wear masks during a pandemic, politicize health and safety, and claim refusal to social distance as a right. Disregard of the safety of others, believing the pandemic is a hoax, or only killing people who need to die anyway, is toxic individualism coupled with numbness to the pain of others. Rage, shame, toxic individualism, and fear will always manifest in one way or another.

Murder Happens in Many Ways

To complicate matters further, our biblical ancestors understood that murder happens in a lot of ways. They quickly realized that it is not simply a biological event. It is perfectly possible to murder a person without inflicting physical harm at all.

According to the *Hebrew and English Lexicon of the Old Testament* (Brown, Driver, and Briggs) the command *lo tirtza-akh* can be understood as: (1) "Don't murder or slay another person or yourself. (2) Don't break, bruise, or crush, which can mean not to break the will of someone or crush his or her spirit. This would apply especially to a child, a spouse, a person who is having financial problems, or a person who can't defend himself or herself. (3) Don't batter or shatter, which can mean not to assault someone physically or verbally and not to humiliate someone."[6] The Talmud contains warnings that humiliating someone or using sneering words is the equivalent of murder. "The person who makes someone else ashamed in the presence of others is as if this person had shed blood."[7] Word Six asks us to refuse to participate in that which is death dealing either to body, soul, or spirit.

The rabbis listed things such as gossip and undue criticism as ways that people murder each other by inflicting grievous harm on the reputation or self-esteem. Someone dear to me once told the story of growing up in a volatile home. As a child he spent a lot of time outside playing in the yard. He loved above all things the large round patch of lily of the valley that his mother had cultivated over the years. One particularly tough day, he was drawn to the lilies. They were fragrant and beautiful. He was so drawn to them that he got into the patch with them. He just wanted to be surrounded by how they made him feel. His mother, spotting him from the kitchen, came out, dragged him from the flowers, beating him handily, and screaming, "You are a bad boy. You are a filthy, filthy, little boy." Something died in him that day. It was something more than his desire to surround himself with fragrant flowers. What died was the little boy who could see them. We can so easily kill with the mouth.

If we take the broad understanding of this word seriously, we see that we kill each other frequently. If we crush a person's spirit, that is murder. If we cause someone to lose their job, that is murder. If we use blame as a weapon and an excuse, that is murder. If we constantly criticize and rarely applaud, that is murder. If we think the work of attaining our goals necessitates taking others down, that is murder. If we fail to nourish when we can, if we withhold affection when we should lavish it, if we feel that we must somehow perfect someone else's offering or win at all costs, that releases kill energy and the smoking gun is in our own hands.

Recently, I was talking to a friend who was grieving the loss of a family member and how the pandemic was cutting her off from her remaining family. In sharing her distress with another friend, that friend told her to buck up, that a lot of people have it worse than she does so she should not complain. She was dashed by this comment, even as she knew that it was true in the big scale of things. She felt guilty for her feelings and began to feel cut off from them. Her friend had no desire to hurt her, yet words that minimize others' feelings and experiences can deal a terrible blow. Pain hurts. It hurts a lot. Just because someone else may hurt more does not mean that the ordinary pains of life do not matter. When we do this to each other, we slowly kill a person's belief in herself or her ability to trust her own experience and find the grace available in it. That is kill energy released as intended kindness. It is really, though, an attempt to control another or to keep one's own hurts safely categorized and neatly put away.

A Call to Community Well-Being

John Calvin expanded the understanding of this Word even further. For him, it was more than an instruction intended to rein in our basest emotions and preserve physical life. He taught that bringing harm to a neighbor in any way was a violation of this Word. He heard in the Sixth Word a call to the believer to see other people's lives as being as precious as one's own.[8]

In that light, the Sixth Word is a call to social justice and community well-being. To refuse to resist structures, patterns, and processes that systematically diminish the life of individuals and groups is a violation of this Word. To allow the hungry to remain hungry, the worker to remain exploited, the vulnerable to be sacrificed, the child to remain in danger, is Murder Most Foul. Even if we are not guilty of causing these ills, per se, if we do nothing to address them, we violate the Word. We can kill directly, and we can kill by apathy or feigned helplessness. Either choice is a violation of this Word.

Sometimes we even take our desire to preserve life (or a way of life) and use kill energy in order to do so. We bomb family planning clinics and kill doctors who work there. All in the name of life and protecting the vulnerable. One of the dangers in this thought process is that we easily come to believe that revenge and retaliation are justified. This belief is often rooted in a misunderstanding of a basic Old Testament concept of an eye for an eye and a tooth for a tooth. This concept of proportionate punishment was an attempt to place boundaries around our need for vengeance while still taking seriously the consequences for wrongdoing. It was actually a step toward mercy in our theological journey. One could no longer kill a person for stealing one's goat. The punishment had to be proportional to the crime. Rather than a rallying cry for revenge, it was a call to sober reflection and even-handed judgment.

The injunction against murder has environmental implications as well. Environmental degradation and disregard damage and kill God's self-expression in the created order and threaten the planet entrusted to our care. As with so many of the evils from which God is trying to protect us in the Ten Words, the most vulnerable will be the first to suffer and the least able to address their suffering in life-sustaining ways. Eventually, the planet itself will struggle to support life and, without intervention and intention, kill energy will have won. Saying "later" or "it is not my problem" or "it doesn't affect me" or "what can I do?" or, worse yet, "God will sovereignly intervene" is not simply a violation of this Word. It is genocide.

We are also masters of non-lethal murder against our own selves. Our negative self-talk and self-destructive habits take a toll. When we perpetuate our pain by ruminating over it to the point that we can see little except through its lens, we crush the life spirit in ourselves. When we see only our failures and inadequacies, we dampen the creative life force. When we tell ourselves we will get moving tomorrow, or eat better tomorrow, or rest a little tomorrow, while we continue to misuse the life of today, we are guilty of murder.

To heal our communities of the kill energy that leads to the violence, anger, and cruelty that so distorts us, we must begin again with personal healing. What we are, our communities are. What we do to ourselves, we will often do to others. What we see in ourselves, we often project onto others. Healing begins with examination. Kill energy nearly always comes from the unconscious. What we do not see we cannot expose to the light for healing. Unexamined attitudes or assumptions about ourselves and others can fester inside of us even telling us that lashing out is good, normal, or necessary. Evil in general, and murder specifically, often succeeds only when disguised as a good.

To counter the capacity to "murder" requires an immersion into the blessedness of life itself. I believe this is why honoring the life givers comes first in the vision that the Ten Words gives us of community life. Life comes first. Do not take it, damage it, or destroy it.

Conclusion

With the Sixth Word, God reaffirms the sacred value of life itself. We are reminded that all life belongs to God and God alone sets the boundaries of it. When we incorporate the deepest meaning of this Word into our lives and commit to live from its truth, we find, in it, an avenue for God to heal our rage, fear, and numbness. Knowing that God asks us to honor life givers and not be life takers, in the next chapter we will consider how we keep our commitments to each other and, in so doing, protect each other's lives.

Spiritual Practice: Examen

Begin your reflection around this Word by creating a space and time to do an *examen*. An examen is a prayer practice that was introduced into the Christian family in the sixteenth century by Ignatius of Loyola, the father of the Jesuit order.

For our purposes, I suggest a slight revision to the traditional examen. Set aside a time for this practice and make a commitment to yourself, and God, to show up and to be present with your whole self to the best of your awareness. Create a space for your examen that is peaceful and calm. You might light a candle or play soothing music. Ask family members for the gift of twenty uninterrupted minutes for you to pray. You may want to pray the examen quietly with your eyes closed or you might want to pray with a journal.

Step One: Ask God to give you light for your reflecting.

Step Two: Give thanks to God for all of your blessings, for every incident of inspiration, healing or kindness. Give thanks for the ways that God fills up the holes in your heart and helps you to move forward. Thank God for your life and all that is life giving in it.

Step Three: Review your day or week. Ask God to show you areas in which you cruelly murder yourself or harm others mindlessly. What dreams, hopes, longings, and feelings have you buried alive? What parts of yourself have you rejected? How do those parts assert themselves at the expense of others? How have you unleashed your tongue like a sword or withheld love and acceptance as a weapon? Have you hurt anyone else? Have you participated in wounding systems or benefited from them in silence?

Step Four: Face your shortcomings. Stay a moment with the feelings you may experience: anger, guilt, confusion, shame. Feel them fully. Face them head-on. Then offer them all to God in a prayer of release.

Step Five: Look to the day to come. Ask God where you will most need God's help in your growth tomorrow, especially in identifying and releasing kill energy. Thank God for this intimate time.

To do the examen, all you need is to honestly show up. You don't have to fix yourself, or even know yourself very well in the beginning. Simply be with God as honestly as you can. Over time, with this practice, compassion, humility, and mercy will replace denial, shame, and rage. We have to know we need mercy to realize its benefits and become dispensers of it. When that happens, the healing has truly begun.

Questions for Personal and Group Reflection

1. What do you see as the most death-dealing realities of our day? Try not to allow this question to take you off into political or ideological tangents. When we do that together we often differ and fall into kill energy toward each other. Think beyond the hot buttons here. What is not supporting love, life, and Spirit in our day?
2. Discuss your understanding of rage and shame. How do you see those dynamics at work in your life and in the world?
3. How do you feel when you hear Jesus say, "turn the other cheek" or "pray for your enemies"?
4. What are the small ways that we "kill" each other mindlessly? Can you think of a specific example?
5. When you think of murder as taking place by the actions we take, and the actions we do not take, what comes to mind? How do you see "passive" murder today?

CHAPTER 7

WORTHY COMPANIONS

Addressing the Core Qualities of Intimacy

You shall not commit adultery.
—Exodus 20:14

Several years ago I spoke at a women's conference at Mo Ranch Conference Center in the beautiful hill country of Texas on the Guadalupe River. It is one of my favorite spots, a "thin place," as the Celts put it, where heaven draws near to earth and the feel of it sparkles in the soul. Back then, the Center had a beautiful aviary filled with exotic and—no less beautiful—ordinary birds. During my down time, I loved to walk in the aviary and see which lovely creatures showed themselves.

One day I arrived when the keeper of the aviary was there. He was tending an unpretentious pair of birds that I had never seen before. They were fairly small, soft pewter in color, with lots of white speckles on their wings. They were diamond wing doves. One of the pair was a little larger. The smaller bird looked very unwell. It was shaking and trembling. Its feathers were going in all directions. I could tell immediately that something was wrong. I asked the keeper about the birds. He said they were wonderfully interesting birds who mate for life. The female of this pair had been attacked by a cat two days before. She was terribly hurt. I asked if she would survive. He was not sure. He said her mate would stay by her side her whole life. If she lived a long time unable to fly, the only time he would leave her would be to get her food and bring her water in his beak. If she lived a short time, he would do the same, crushing up seeds for her, opening her beak to put the mush in. No matter what life had done to her, and no matter how she responded, he would never leave her side.

That little picture in nature gives us a glimpse of how God is with us. It also gives us a look at what God's intention is for marriage. In sickness and in health as long as we both shall live. Sadly, it is not always a picture of human behavior.

So far in the Ten Words, God has established that life in its fullest is the highest value of the beloved community. With the Seventh Word, we turn to consider ways that life can be stolen or adulterated. Again, we begin with the family.

On a snowy afternoon years ago, I sat at my desk in the church, engrossed in preparing a Bible study. I was alone in the building that afternoon when the bell on the back door rang. I went to the door to find a parishioner named Ed (not his real name) standing there in his faded work clothes. Ed was in his late thirties, a burly blue-collar worker with large hands and an even larger heart.

Ed was married to a woman who had a very difficult history. She was much younger, as I recall, and had been living on the streets off and on when Ed met her. He saw something beautiful in her and fell head over heels. Several months earlier, his wife had had a miscarriage. It undid her. She had never trusted that anyone would really love her and had wanted a child because, she said, "The baby will have to love me."

After the miscarriage, Ed tried everything he could to comfort and support her, but nothing worked. Very quickly she turned to drugs and other men to quell the pain momentarily. This only made matters worse. She couldn't stop. Nor could she escape the disgust she felt toward herself. So almost every day she confessed to Ed and begged for forgiveness. Then the next. Then the next.

The day he came to the church, Ed had come home from work to find her packing. "I'm leaving," she said. "I can't even bear your forgiveness anymore." I remember Ed putting his head in his hands and saying, "Why? Why doesn't my love make a difference?"

That is the pain from which God is trying to protect us in the Seventh Word.

Statistics regarding adultery in the United States are notoriously hard to get. People are reluctant to admit to it. According to the website divorcestatistics.info, estimates are that around a quarter of men and somewhat fewer women admit to straying in their marriages. Among younger people, the estimates are higher. Fear of a spouse finding out is the biggest factor in reining in behavior, with up to 60 percent of people saying they would have an affair if they were sure it would never be discovered.

Adultery in the Bible

In the world of the Old Testament, adultery was understood to be a grievous sin and a capital crime. But what exactly was adultery? Adultery in the Bible was sexual intercourse to completion between a married woman and any man other than her husband. There was not even an exemption for rape. The woman was still an adulteress. Other forms of sexual activity were exempt.

Married men were not bound by sexual fidelity. They were free to have sex with unmarried women and, in doing so, the unmarried women became a secondary wife or concubine. This behavior was considered honorable. Polygamy was common in the Old Testament and understood as a sign of prosperity and blessing from God. King Solomon had 300 wives and 700 concubines and was deemed wise and faithful (1 Kgs. 11:3)! Married men, however, were forbidden from having sex with women married to other men. This was understood as a crime against her husband *and* against God.

Marriage in the ancient world was rarely solely a matter of romantic love, although there are beautiful love stories in the Bible. Marriages were economic unions and family partnerships that were crucial for the survival of the tribe and the community. Parents negotiated matches, with or without consultation with their children. The bonds of marriage between families transcended death. If a husband died without children, his brother took his widow as a wife to raise children in the dead brother's name.

The prohibition against adultery was not about sex per se. The issue was paternity. A man needed to be sure that his children were his own. Without that security, the promise given to Abraham and Sarah of descendants as many as the stars was rendered null and void. The Jewish philosopher and student of Scripture, Philo of Alexandria, emphasized this point saying, "The deceived husband is like a blind man knowing nothing of the covert intrigues of the past yet forced to cherish the children of his deadliest foe as his own flesh and blood."[1]

At issue was the man's and the family's future, both now and after his death. Our early Jewish ancestors believed that this life was God's gift to us. After death, we lived on through our children and our children's children. To break the line of paternity was to lose hope of eternity. Extinction of the family line was extinction of the promise itself.

While there is scholarly debate as to whether, or how often, the death penalty was actually carried out for adultery, the fact that it is clearly stated in the legal codes demonstrates how seriously they took this instruction. Both partners in the act were considered guilty and worthy of death. Descriptions of the consequences, however, focus on the woman. For her execution, she was to be publicly stripped from the waist up and either forced to drink poison, cast into a ravine, burned to death, or stoned. Whether those penalties were routinely enforced or not, it is clear that the sanctity of the family lay at the heart of Israel's moral understanding.

Adultery was also viewed as a property crime. It was the stealing of a man's property—his wife—and the misuse of it by another man. This aspect of the crime could be why this Word is placed where it is in most of the manuscripts, paired with the Eighth Word, which prohibits stealing. In a few codices this Word appears as the Sixth Word, paired with honoring the life givers as a way of beginning all of community life with preservation of the family.

A part of the seriousness with which this behavior was taken had to do with the understanding of adultery, not just as a crime against the husband, but as a direct crime against God. The midrash taught that God officiated at the first marriage in the garden of Eden, thereby making clear that marriage was to be honored and that God had a stake in all marriages.[2] It is the family and the tribe through which God desires blessing to flow to all people and the whole created order. Families are not just where *we* are loved. They are intended to be the vehicles through which God pours love into the whole human family. This Word reminds us that nothing should be allowed to truncate that love outpouring.

The Hebrew language helps us to see the sacred quality of our unions. The word for the engagement period, a time when a couple was pledged to marriage, but the bride still lived at home, is *kuddushin*. It is from the root, *kadosh* which means "holy" or "set apart for a godly purpose." The word for marriage, *nisuin*, means "uplifting." By implication, to violate those commitments is to choose ungodliness and to tear down rather than to uplift.

God's Voice or Our Own?

The Old Testament prophets used the metaphor of adultery to talk about Israel's faithfulness to God. Hosea, in particular, uses his own broken family life as a metaphor for the entire community's unwillingness to love and commit to God alone. In other words, what happens in our homes happens in the broader community. If we are not faithful to our partners, we learn to not value faithfulness in any situation when to remain faithful is inconvenient or unpleasant.

When offering us the Seventh Word, God knew that if we are not faithful to our partners and others, it becomes difficult for us to hear from God, let alone be faithful to God. The siren call of our egos can drown out God's voice and our own common sense. The ego has the uncanny ability to convince us that anything we want is good for us and that anything that feels right, must be acceptable to God.

Back in the 1980s, I had a young teenager in my youth group. One evening the group was talking about choices and how we make them. This young woman said, "I trust my gut. If it feels right it must be right. If I am convinced that it is right, that makes it right." I was aghast and pushed back a little. "Do you mean to tell me that if I got a 357 Magnum, pointed it at your head, convinced without a shadow of a doubt that I was right, and pulled the trigger, that would make it right?" "Yes," she said. Granted, she was probably trying to wind me up. She succeeded, too. Deciding that something is right because it feels right is the very reasoning that lies at the heart of many a ruined marriage. If we think that what we want is necessarily right because it feels so good that it must be willed by God or at least morally neutral, then we can easily discount the pain we unleash. When this way of evaluating moral choices becomes our standard, we can quickly find that all of our commitments and boundaries are also porous and dependent entirely on our perceptions of what feels right in the moment—even our commitment to God!

In the Hebrew Scriptures, faithfulness is generally given to God. All faithfulness to others and to the community is a way of demonstrating faithfulness to God. In Hosea's vision, we are wed to God. It is God's own faithfulness that has been implanted in human beings so that we can then reflect that faithfulness back to God. Marriage, in that sense, is a laboratory for learning who we are and how to be faithful to God in all things.

The central image for faithfulness is covenant. Covenants are mutually binding agreements to which all parties commit. Covenants were said to be cut or carved as a way to express their permanence. They are inviolable. God's central covenant with humanity is that God will be our God and we will be God's people. The Ten Words, called the Covenant of the Law, outline the agreements within the covenant of God's love. We may stray from this agreement, but God will not. When we stray from our agreements, we lose sight both of God and who we are in relation to God.

A number of years ago, a young man in my parish got into trouble. He was a beautiful young man, raised in the church by loving parents who were faith-filled people. In his late teens he got involved with drugs, got arrested for dealing, and wound up in state prison. One day I drove up to the prison to see him. We had to visit through plexiglass shields and talk to each other through phone headsets. I had not been to a state prison before and I was pretty shaken up by the whole scene. When the young man came in, orange jumpsuit and shackles, mop of blonde hair and impossible blue eyes, I was so overwhelmed that the first words out of my mouth were, "Jimmy, what are you doing here?" Without a missed beat he said, "Pastor, I am here to find out who I am not."

The Seventh Word invites us to find out who we are not. The "thou shalt nots" are God's loving invitation to us to cut away that which can never serve us, can never take our faith deeper, can never heal our wounds, reveal our true selves, or stabilize our communities.

Worthy Companions

If, then, faithlessness is *not* who we are, then who are we intended to be in our most intimate relationships? In the second creation story in the book of Genesis (2.4b), God, after the wild burst of creative frenzy, forms a human being from the dust of the ground, breathing life into it. At that moment the creature, called Adam in English translations, a Word that means "earth creature" or "creature made of earth," is genderless. The earth creature does not initially have a partner. God's intent seems to have been that God would be the consort of this creature. As is so often the case with human beings, God was not enough for the earth creature. It became miserably lonely.

When God looks at the loneliness of the first human, God is moved with compassion and decides to make a particular kind of companion for it. The Hebrew phrase used in the text, *ezer kenegdo*, is difficult to translate. The old King James version translates it as "help meet." That falls far short of the real meaning of the word. Fit companion, worthy companion, corresponding companion, all of those are ways that biblical scholars have tried to express the meaning of the term. The *ezer kenegdo* is the one in whose presence we are safe to become all that God has dreamed for us to be. *Ezer kenegdo* relationships are marked by fidelity, safety, mutuality, trust, and generativity. *Ezer kenegdo* relationships, as a matter of will, choose not to manipulate, coerce, attempt to fix, dominate, or demean the partner. In *ezer kenegdo* relationships, we are safe to be who we are. We are always encouraged to grow. In these relationships, the well-being of the other carries equal weight to one's own and greater weight than any other momentary desires.

This is God's original intention for marriage. Safety. Intimacy. Mutuality. Fidelity. Joy. These core qualities are not possible in an atmosphere of betrayal, porous boundaries, and insincere commitment.

The question can certainly be asked whether every marriage is really a reflection of this sacred intention. Are we bound by commitments if they were coerced? Are we bound by commitments if our partners are not, or if they are abusive either physically or emotionally? Those are difficult questions that have given rise in the Catholic Church to the theology of annulment. In some circumstances, the church judges that no actual marriage took place. Even if the rituals are rightly performed, sometimes things go horribly awry. In that case, partners are freed from their commitments. Protestants have largely rejected that theology, but do recognize that not all marriages are lived out in a sacred way and some, to preserve life and sanity, must end. Even so, we recognize that that is far from God's original intention for us. God simply never wants us to hurt that badly.

Adultery's threat to community went beyond the pain and dissolution of intimacy in the family. It even went beyond the threat to the promise itself. The ancestors recognized that when vows are not sacrosanct and boundaries are not respected in one area of life, they are easily disrespected in other areas. If spouses cannot be trusted to honor their partners, can they be trusted to faithfully carry the values of the community? The ability to make a commitment to the good of others, apart from our own personal desires, is what keeps communities from devolving into chaos.

The prohibition against adultery asks us to consider what we are willing to do to another person, and who we are willing to hurt, to get what we think we want. The ancestors recognized that when we choose to make our desires the sole basis for decision making and ethics, we cannot keep families, communities, or the beloved community on an even keel.

Jesus' Broad View

In teaching about the dangers of adultery, Jesus broadens the prohibition to include the ways we think, as well as how we behave. "You have heard that it was said, 'You shall not commit adultery.' But I say to you that everyone who looks at a woman with lust has already committed adultery with her in his heart" (Matt. 5:27–28). Jesus recognized that what we are willing to entertain in our minds can easily become a lived reality. It doesn't have to, but it can. The word adultery itself can help us see how.

The word adultery in English comes from a Latin root that means "to water down" or "to debase something by using cheap materials." I once heard a pastor preaching on this passage use the example of brewing tea. He talked about how adding too much water to the tea made the tea lose all of its character and distinctiveness. He went on to explore the layers that we add onto our relationships that cheapen them and make them unrecognizable as the sacred vehicles they are intended to be.

Adultery rarely springs up from nowhere. It can happen only when a partner feels a need for something that is not being met and thinks that it can somehow be met in the arms of another. The need may have little or nothing to do with the marriage and everything to do with unrecognized wounds in the individual that no partner could ever heal. Unless that deep and difficult inner work is attempted, no relationships are safe.

For others, the issues that lead to straying may lie in the relationship itself. The question then becomes, how do we water down or cheapen our marriages to such an extent that they can no longer bear the weight of life and fidelity? Clearly we can do that in ways in addition to sexual infidelity.

We can begin to identify those ways if we consider the core qualities of *ezer kenegdo*. The first of these values is safety. Obviously, this kind of relationship cannot exist in an atmosphere of physical danger or the threat of it. A friend once told me about how frightened she was of her husband. He had never struck her or verbally threatened to do so. She said, though, that he menaced her. She was a small woman and he was a large man. She said that sometimes she would be in the kitchen trying to prepare a family meal and he would come in enraged for some reason and just follow her around the kitchen in a seething silence. He corralled her at the sink or stove, trapping her against cabinets until she sometimes sank to the floor crying, "I'm so sorry," when she never even knew what she was apologizing for.

Threats to safety can be more subtle than that. If a partner realizes that there are taboo subjects that can never be addressed, if a tight rein is kept on finances, if a partner constantly questions where the other partner has been, verbally demeans or ridicules, there can be little question of safety in the relationship.

Intimacy, or true bonding, requires that both partners are committed to their own growth and development in the context of the relationship. True intimacy rejoices in the other and stamps out jealousy or competition in the relationship. True intimacy creates spaces for the other to blossom. The Bohemian-Austrian poet, Rainer Maria Rilke put it this way,

> A good marriage is that in which each appoints the other guardian of his solitude. . . . Once the realization is accepted that even between the closest human beings infinite distances continue to exist, a wonderful living side-by-side can grow up, if they succeed in loving the distance between them which makes it possible for each to see the other whole against a wide sky.[3]

Intimacy such as this not only gives permission for partners to be their truest selves, it relishes, rejoices, and praises it. When partners come to believe that the other is somehow holding them back or trying to put them in a box of expectations, relationships deteriorate. *Ezer kenegdo* relationships rest on mutuality and agreements not to thwart the other's emerging.

Sometimes we water down, or cheapen, our relationships by becoming so busy and so earnest in our endeavors that there is little room left for joy and laughter. Every long-lasting marriage I've ever seen has been filled with laughter. Laughing together at a joke, a movie, or just the absurdity of life is a powerful aphrodisiac and great preventive medicine. Sharing laughter with a trusted partner creates bonds that are hard to break.

Honoring All Our Vows

The Seventh Word is all about relationships and the deep commitments that we make to those closest to us. Of course it is about sexual fidelity in marriage, but it is also about fidelity period. This Word asks us to think carefully about the commitments and promises that we make in every arena of life and to honor them as inviolable.

Vows can be adulterated and betrayed in families, communities, and churches with painful consequences. A colleague of mine tells the story of such violations inflicted from and within the church in her book *With Scars on My Soul: A Story of Release and Redemption.*[4] In this novel, she tells the story of a pastor who started a new pastorate with great hope, joy, and a deep sense of calling. The underlying issues and secrets in that congregation led to the dissolution of the pastoral relationship fairly quickly. The promises the congregation made to her at her installation were joyfully kept by the majority, but the minority set in motion events that could never be resolved. The result was pain and heartache for many, and a church lost and dying because of its unwillingness to honor its vows, look honestly at its life, and go to God for healing.

While that is an extreme example of how a system, or a family, can come apart when people cannot keep faith with our sacred vows to nourish and protect each other, we do that in many ways and contexts. When we don't keep our covenants as a human family, we carry the scars on our souls. That pain leaks into the church, from the church, and the whole culture is increasingly poisoned by our inability to be faithful to each other. When we fail to stay true to the vows we make in small things, it is easier to do that in larger things and the pain then gets into the very water table of human life and we all drink the bitter water.

Sometimes we even begin to think that that is what water tastes like, and we are no longer scandalized.

The Seventh Word is a caution to *each* of us about our covenant relationship and responsibility toward *all* of us. We are one human family, bound together in ways that go beyond, and are deeper, than borders or cultures. Just by breathing in and out in the world we make commitments to each other. Just by breathing, we vow that we will, insofar as we are able, be there for each other, for better and worse, richer and poorer, in sickness and in health. We must not allow our selfish momentary needs to break those vows.

When I apply that lens to this Word, I can see very quickly that we do not, as individuals or as a culture, always honor this vow. There are many examples. We in the United States have violated every treaty ever signed with the native nations upon whose lands we now live. We have pulled out of climate accords intended to help many nations make way for the earth to heal from decades of neglect. During the coronavirus pandemic, experts encouraged simple health practices, such as masks and distancing, to save lives and prevent suffering, and yet people held mask burning parties intended to transmit the virus and continued to say that COVID-19 is just like the flu. Then they went about their lives, unprotected, while states fought for ventilators and set up refrigeration trucks outside hospitals as makeshift morgues. Through these types of selfish actions, we break our vows to each other and declare that what we want when we want it is more important than those who might be harmed by our actions. It is that very dynamic of disregard that lies at the heart of the Seventh Word.

Let's look at it from the other side as well. Every day that we make choices, every time that we set aside our preferences or natural inclinations, for the good of others, we honor this Word. With my lungs and immune system being compromised, Robbie took on the job of my defender, protector, and bodyguard in those pandemic days, not letting anyone near me who could potentially transmit the virus. One morning, however, we had to have a workman in the house to fix an electrical problem. We were grateful to see how this man honored the unspoken vow we take as a human family. When he came to the door, I told him I was immune challenged and asked him to put on gloves and a mask before he came in the house. I apologized for his inconvenience. His response was, "Keeping you safer is worth it to me." He stood on the front porch, left his toolbox there, and put on protective gear before he came in to examine our issue. I felt seen, respected, and honored in that small human transaction. This stranger kept his vow.

Forgiveness

Grace and forgiveness are needed if we are to heal from the blows that others' violation of this Word can land on our hearts and souls. Dealing with violations of this Word can be extremely painful, especially in our marriages. Feelings of betrayal can be devastating for both the betrayed and the betrayer. Forgiving is the only way forward, even if the relationship is beyond repair.

Many strong marriages are able to withstand and grow through experiences of betrayal. Others are not. In either case, damage is done, and scars remain, often for a lifetime.

My Aunt Gladys was born in the waning years of the nineteenth century in the small town of Pineapple, Alabama. She was born into a wealthy family of cotton farmers, former plantation owners who still managed the land in the decades after the Civil War. She was very proud of her lineage, which included the author Nathaniel Hawthorne—the author of the novel *The Scarlet Letter*, all about the ravages adultery leaves in its wake. Aunt Gladys lived her entire life in the old plantation house with the wide veranda, eighteen-foot ceilings, and the third-floor ballroom. The house still stands, a shadow of its former self.

Aunt Gladys grew up a belle but not a stereotypical one. She was wild and outspoken and known to curse shockingly and with a great deal of relish. In the 1920s she married a man I only ever heard her refer to as Captain Whitaker. By all reports, he was a charismatic and rakish man who enjoyed Aunt Gladys' society connections.

In those days, young women of means often took their summers together in Paris to escape the intense heat of Alabama. The men stayed home and conducted whatever business they had, met to drink whiskey and go shooting, and generally enjoy a bit of freedom. One summer, while Aunt Gladys was in Paris, Captain Whitaker's business seemed to be the local piano teacher. He absconded with her, leaving only a note and never returning to Alabama again.

By the time I spent any time with Aunt Gladys, fifty years had passed. She never remarried, and as far as anyone remembers, she nursed her hurt and the hatred that grew from it every day for the rest of her life. She never passed up an opportunity to tell anyone who would listen what a rat Captain Whitaker was. She died seventy years after the blow, living in one room of the old house, which she could not afford to heat, and had no one to leave it to. She never recovered and she missed out on life.

In the Bible, forgiveness is understood as the wiping out of an offense and its penalty. In the case of God, forgiveness extends to God wiping out the very memory of the offense (Isa. 43:25). God does this so that what happened no longer has power to condition the relationship. Forgiveness can only be given by the victim. It can't be given on behalf of the victim. Since all sin is seen as an offense against God, God forgives as the victim.

When thinking about the deepest wounds we sustain from those closest to us, it is important to remember that forgiveness is a choice and not a feeling. It is also true that it is easier to say than to do. It takes time to let go of a past that cannot be changed. Even then, forgiveness does not remove the scars, but it can change the way we view the scars. A forgiven memory, unless you are God, is not a deleted memory nor does it mean we pretend that things are not the way they are, or that it wasn't that bad to begin with. Forgiveness is God's way of dealing with our pain and we only do it when we decide we don't want to hurt anymore.

Forgiveness of self and others when we have violated our commitments, especially in our deepest relationships, changes the lens through which we see our lives and the world. Years ago, when I was going through the dark days of divorce, a dear colleague gave me a cross that had been given to her during a dark time in her life. The cross is made from two spent shell casings from a firearm. In the cross bar there is a tiny hole to look inside. Inside the casings is a beautiful kaleidoscope of multicolored gems. My friend told me that the cross symbolized that, even things that can do the worst damage, when viewed through the lens of the cross, can be transformed into something of great beauty. She told me that when I didn't need it anymore, I was to pass it along to someone who did. I still wear it.

Conclusion

When I was in seminary and it came time to study this Word in my Old Testament class, my professor read the Word aloud to us and paused for a long moment. He had gone on at length about the other Words, but this time he was silent. Finally he said, "Just don't do it. All hell will break loose if you do." We all laughed but he summed it all up in those few words. The Seventh Word reminds us that adultery is not just about who is doing what with whom behind closed doors. It is more fundamentally about who and what we are willing to harm in order to get what we think we want or to meet a need we don't know how else to meet. When we choose to make others' lives and feelings subject to our own unexamined desires, we create pain that destroys families, poisons churches, and leaves the community at risk. Adultery, in its strictest and its broadest sense, sows chaos and robs people of a future. In the next chapter we will examine other ways we steal from each other.

Spiritual Practice: Praying for Forgiveness or to Forgive

In *The Book of Forgiving*, Desmond and Mpho Tutu offer a number of practices to help with facing and freeing the heart from the deepest wounds. The following meditation practice was inspired by their work.

1. Set a time of at least twenty minutes to reflect. Ask those around you to give you the uninterrupted time as a gift. Take several deep calming breaths, remembering that even your breathing is a prayer of receiving the Spirit and releasing that which does not serve your growth.

2. Imagine that you are in a beautiful safe place and Jesus is with you. Take a few moments to feel the warmth and safety of his presence. Thank him for being with you in this journey. Ask him to guide you to the insight and healing you most need.

3. Imagine now that you are standing in front of a wall covered with safety deposit boxes. Jesus has a large ring with the keys to those boxes. Each box contains the memory of a hurt you have received, or one that you have

inflicted. They each contain only one and are labeled so you know what is in each.

4. Imagine that Jesus asks you to choose a box/memory/situation that you would like to examine in his presence. Choose a box and ask Jesus to open it for you to look into.

5. Inside are all the memories and feelings that you have stored about this incident. Ask Jesus to shed light on each one. Ask for forgiveness for yourself if needed. If you are ready to forgive, then offer the contents of the box to Jesus for him to dispose of as is best for all involved. If it is too hard or unbearable, simply close the box. You can return when you are ready. Choosing a box and giving a first look is pleasing to God and you will be strengthened for the next prayer time.

6. As you go forward with emptying the box, remove the label when you are done and put the box back in the wall. It is ready to be filled with new and loving memories now. You do not need it anymore. You are free and can let it go.

7. Before you open your eyes, take a moment to fully breathe in the presence of Christ. Thank God for accompanying you and releasing you.

8. Take a few moments to write about your experience. Close your prayer time with a few minutes of gratitude for all the gifts of your life, especially for the power to forgive and the grace of receiving forgiveness.

Questions for Personal and Group Reflection

1. What are the most important commitments that human beings make to one another?
2. Do you think there is still a double standard in how women and men experience the consequences of adultery?

3. How do you think this Word speaks to conversations about sexual misconduct?
4. In what ways do you think people water down their commitments? Can you think of specific times when you have watered down an important relationship without it being sexual?
5. Discuss the concept of *ezer kenegdo*. How have you experienced this in your life? In what ways might you nurture these types of relationships in your home or congregation?

CHAPTER 8

TO CATCH A THIEF

Addressing Theft from God,
Self, and Community

You shall not steal.
—Exodus 20:15

Stealing is a familiar concept. The headlines are full of stories of money managers who abscond with funds, of celebrities who walk out of upscale boutiques having "forgotten" to pay, and people doing time in jail for stealing a six pack from the 7-Eleven. Images of looting after natural disasters or protests often define those events in the minds of those who observe from a distance.

Perhaps we are personally familiar with a little thieving. The ream of paper that winds up in our briefcases from the office, the library book that has been on our shelf for thirty years, the bill we meant to pay before we left town—all of these are common. Only rarely do they produce lasting feelings of guilt.

When I was in college, I drove to my hometown to visit my parents (and do my laundry) about once a month. In those days, the two-lane highways between Greenville and Tuscaloosa wound through woods and farmland that was sparsely populated. About halfway on the journey, there was a crossroads with a small country store and gas station. The store was most notable because it sold fresh Krispy Kreme donuts, a regional treat to this day.

Often on my way back to campus on a Sunday afternoon, I stopped at the store to buy donuts to take to the fraternity where I was a little sister. Never one to shun buying affection, this became a bit of a routine. One Sunday, I must have been flush with cash because I bought three dozen of the donuts for "the fellas." For myself, I wanted a pack of Dentyne chewing gum and a soft drink. I remember the balancing act of getting the boxes of donuts and drink to the cash register and the relief I felt when I got to the car without dumping everything on the gravel parking lot.

I drove on blissfully thinking about the coming week. Everything was fine until I reached into my pocket for a tissue and withdrew the pack of gum. I realized that in my effort to get things to the counter safely, I had tucked the gum in my pocket and forgotten to pay for it. I was horrified. I broke out into a sweat. I was a thief.

By this point I had driven thirty miles past the store. Should I turn back? Finally my discomfort became too much for me. I turned back. When I got to the store and told the cashier what had happened, handing him my shame-soaked quarter, he looked at me like I had two heads. "You drove all the way back here for a quarter," he said shaking his head and ringing up the sale. "I couldn't come up with a good enough reason not to," I replied.

I've thought of that little episode often over the years. I must admit, that there have been plenty of times in later life, that I have found good enough reasons to live with a little less integrity than this Word invites.

Personal Property and More

In the beloved community, there is no stealing. In part, this prohibition is intended to protect personal property. We do not take what does not belong to us. At the same time, it is a little more complicated. These Words are first given to people wandering in the wilderness looking for home. In the early years of the exodus, all of the people would have been former slaves who had very little personal property. (Though apparently they had some, because the women had jewelry, given to them by the Egyptian women (Exod. 12:35–36) that could be melted down to make the golden calf.) Was this Word about God's desire that the people not take from each other the little that they had? Did God see among them potential jewelry, quail, and manna thieves? To complicate things further, they would soon be sent across the Jordan River to claim a land that others already claimed as their own. Why this Word to those people at that time? Was thieving in the eye of the beholder?

The issue of personal ownership in Israel was always nuanced. Yes, people had claim to their possessions and the goods of their trades and shops. But not really. God was the actual owner of everything. The land and all goods were gifts from God, and temporary ones at that. God's people were stewards of the land and goods *for* God. Everything belonged to God and was to be used to further God's ends. To steal was to steal from God. By implication, to take at God's direction was God's own doing with God's own possessions. That understanding undergirded the conquest of the land. God had promised it. It was God's to give, so it was faithfulness to claim it. Sadly, believing that one is chosen by God and therefore acting for God, has been used to justify crusades, colonization, and genocides for centuries.

The Old Testament prophets railed against the ways that Israel stole what rightfully belonged to God. They accused the community of robbing widows' houses, failing to provide for orphans, and withholding tithes and offerings that were due to God. Malachi saw withholding one's tithe as robbing God directly and believed it to be a cause of the breakdown of the community itself. To rob God of what God owns or asks, or to withhold the good God desires, is to shut off the flow of blessing to both the perpetrator and the community.

Rabbi Isaac Klein illustrates this point.

> Whatever we have, we only hold in stewardship, in trust from God. It is significant that there is no word in Hebrew for beggars or alms. The Hebrew equivalent, *tzedakah*, which we say when talking about giving to the poor, actually means righteousness or right doing. According to our doctrine, the poor have a right to be supported by those who are more fortunate because the more fortunate are only stewards for what belongs to God.[1]

The Hebrew of the Eighth Word, *lo tig-nove*, has as its root the word *gonab*. This word usually means to take from another by stealth or undercover. We can see the evolution of understanding of the Word by looking at how it evolved in Yiddish.[2] In Yiddish, the word *gonnif* meant thief. It also carried a quality of cleverness or the capacity to outwit a bureaucracy that was stacked against a person. Whether the word referred to someone who hurt people by stealing from them, or someone who was clever and looked out for her or others' interests by deceit, was conveyed by tone of voice and facial expression. What kind of *gonnif* was Robin Hood? It depends on who is telling the story.

In Genesis 27 we see this struggle played out in our faith family. Jacob, the younger twin of Isaac, conspires with his mother Rebekah to gain his dying father's all-important last blessing. His father, whose eyesight has failed him, is nearing the end of his life and wants to put his affairs in order. Jacob dresses in his brother's clothes and goes to the old man to gain his blessing. The deception works. It also sets in motion events, and family estrangement, that persists for generations. Jacob got what he wanted, but at a cost.

While the line is sometimes dotted, the Eighth Word warns us that there is a line between stealing and dealing. In addition to honoring the property of others, this Word cautions against deceit in general. The use of lies or manipulation to convince another of something that is only to the deceiver's benefit, was considered a grievous moral wrong and a violation of the Eighth Word. There is an old expression in the Southern United States that captures this truth simply. "If you scratch a liar, you'll find a thief."

The recognition of the human tendency to take advantage by deceptive dealing or unfair business practices gave rise to a need to balance the books as a community. Every seventh year a sabbatical year was proclaimed. In Leviticus 25, this year is called a sabbath to God. During sabbatical years the land was given a rest from production, debts were forgiven, and the enslaved were set free. After the seventh cycle of sabbatical years, jubilee was declared. The releases and forgiveness of this sabbatical year were expanded to restore all land to its original owners (original Israelite owners, at least) if those owners had been forced to sell it out of economic need. The steadfast belief that the land ultimately belonged to God and could not be sold underlay these practices. Families and tribes were set up by God and were always mere guests upon the land (Lev. 25:23). The understanding was that to profit from selling the land at the expense of those to whom God had bestowed it was to steal from God.

A Social Crime

Early in Israel's theological reflection on the Eighth Word, the rabbis understood the prohibition against stealing in much the way that we today understand kidnapping. Not only are we not to steal a person's possessions, we are not to steal their lives, freedom, or reputation. We are not to steal people to sell them into slavery, to coerce their work, or to gain wealth by exploiting them. To do so carried the death penalty (Deut. 24:7). Israel never forgot slavery in Egypt, and quickly understood this Word to forbid exploiting people for economic gain.

Stealing was a social crime that affected all of the community. In the beloved community, we do not steal by taking what is not ours either personally or systemically. Patrick Miller explains it this way:

> The Eighth Commandment thus does not simply inhibit one from mugging a person on the street or robbing a bank. . . . It also serves to effect a more systemic activity to ensure the economic sufficiency of one's neighbor, a systemic activity that is not even vulnerable to likes and dislikes, favoritisms and antipathies, to hostilities and enmity between members of the community.[3]

We are not to rob people of a chance to make a living or survive.

At the heart of this Word is God's desire that all of God's children have what they need in order to live a dignified life full of blessing. In the beloved community we do not take from anyone that which makes a life of dignity possible. That includes one's possessions but — much more profoundly — a person's capacity to thrive, their personal power and self-esteem.

As with murder, stealing can be active and passive. We steal from others by the choices we make and the behaviors that those choices engender. Economic systems that exploit workers violate this Word. Examples of wage theft by owners and managers who falsify time sheets or miscalculate wages is not uncommon with farm workers who do not speak English or who cannot read or write. That is but one example of theft disguised as good for business.

The charging of excessive interest is another form of economic stealing. For workers who do not earn a living wage and live from paycheck to paycheck, loans against next week's pay often charge exorbitant interest or fees for check cashing that leave hard-working, low-wage workers unable to ever dig out. Usury, or charging excessive interest, is roundly condemned in the Old Testament in numerous passages (see Ps. 15; Ezek. 18:14–17 for examples). There are some passages in which interest is allowed to be charged to foreigners but never to fellow Israelites. In short, when we exploit in any way, we steal.

Ways We Steal

We also steal by the choices we do not make. We steal with our voices and we steal with our silence. We do it as individuals and we do it as societies. The Eighth Word asks us to consider what we take from and what we give to others with our personal actions and with actions with which we are silently complicit.

The way we tell the stories of history can give to others or steal from them. History exists in the lens of the one who tells the story. If all we see in the founding stories of United States history are the conquerors and their noble ideals, then we rob ourselves—and especially the conquered—of the truth and with it our capacity to understand the present and address its challenges. If we see the first peoples of the land as pagan savages that had to be exterminated, we write history in one way. If we see the same peoples as freedom fighters trying to protect their homes and cultures, we write history in a different way. Both views are in some ways reductionist. The former, however, allows for the theft of land, culture, and identity and gives a basis for treaty breaking in order to exploit the richness of the land to benefit those who claimed it but did not own it.

White supremacy is an example of wholesale cultural theft. The powerfully reinforced belief that whiteness is superior and normative in society steals from everyone. If we are white, it steals our self-understanding and even our capacity to entertain the notion that we do not know what we do not know. If we are people of color, it steals our access to goods, upward mobility, cultures, dignity, and our own voices.

The toll of this theft is both material and psychological. It is soul crushing for both thief and victim. The victims of perpetual theft of dignity can come to collude with the theft and believe that they either deserve it or at least can hope for no better.

We also see the theft of dignity and its erosion of self in syndromes like battered spouse syndrome. Verbal and physical abuse can leave a spouse immobilized and full of self-blame. "I shouldn't have parked the car crookedly." "He really does love me. I'm just hard to live with." "She deserves better than me." This is not only theft of human dignity and a threat to human life, it also robs God of the fulfillment of God's desires for both victim and victimizer.

We can even steal with good, but unexamined intentions. The Black Lives Matter movement gives a perfect example of this. When white people counter that movement with All Lives Matter, or Police Lives Matter, that is to miss the point. Those phrases, while obviously true, steal the reality that not all lives are equally vulnerable to toxic economics and police brutality. For those of us who are white to claim that we do not see color may be well-meaning, but still misses the mark. To not see color is a way of making everyone an "honorary white person." It conveys that we do not want to listen and receive all the gifts that they bring to our lives and community. It also says that we are not interested in the critique that comes when truth is honestly shared. That robs even a well-intentioned person of the benefit of knowing their own reality more fully. With the Eighth Word we learn that it doesn't matter if we do not consciously intend harm. We often do harm anyway and when we do, we steal.

Cultural appropriation is another example of theft. Several years ago, I was privileged to work with a ministry with and for the empowerment and protection of indigenous people in our area of California. One of the aspects of our work was a literacy program for mothers and their babies, most of whom still spoke their indigenous languages. The moms wanted their children to be ready for school, so we worked with reading and learning activities to help them develop tri-lingual language skills.

In the course of that work, our project director, an indigenous woman whose home tribe had lived in the Americas for 8,000 years, told me one of the sacred stories of her people. It was the story of how the rabbit got into the moon. I was enthralled. I had a dream of creating a beautiful picture book of this story using artwork from the children in our program. I wanted that story to become a part of the broader experience of the community.

In my zeal, I wrote a children's book about the story. I was so excited when I sent it to my friend, the director, for critique. When I did not get a response for three days, I knew that I had done something wrong. After a few more days she wrote me a careful letter showing me how what I had done was cultural appropriation. In my whiteness and with my good intentions, I had taken what was not mine and made it my own without the soul knowledge and lived experience to give the story its sacred power. I recognized my theft as soon as I read her email and deleted the story from my hard drive. I apologized and thanked her for being my friend and helping me see more clearly. I stole. She gave. When we mindlessly appropriate the cultures of native peoples for our sports teams or business enterprises, we steal that which is unique and sacred from people for our own amusement. We may say it is harmless fun, or even that it somehow honors, but that simply adds lies to theft.

Understanding how our actions give to and take from others is the loving urge at the heart of the Eighth Word. It doesn't have to be as dramatic. We steal from each other with unkind words, sometimes masked as humor. In her book *White Fragility*, sociologist Robin Diangelo cites a study of college students who, in general, profess to not be racist. Students were asked to keep a journal for one week of every racial issue, image, or understanding that they observed. They asked this of 626 college students in twenty-eight universities around the country. In that one week the students recorded more than seventy-five hundred racist comments, many in the form of jokes, or told sheepishly with slurs. Rarely were the comments or jokes challenged.[4] Perhaps no one from the targeted groups heard these jokes, but they were still harmed because the jokes themselves, and not confronting them, reinforce white solidarity. They reinforce the perception that people of color are somehow "other" that need to be kept in their place. These things, both spoken and unchallenged, can be grand theft.

Stealing Subtly

There are more subtle ways that we violate this Word as well. Richard Levy writes that this Word includes the prohibition against keeping people waiting, because when we do so we steal their time. We imply by this that they are not worth our effort to be on time and in so doing steal a bit of their self-esteem and dignity. The Word prohibits not giving credit to authors for their ideas. It prohibits misleading flattery because it steals some of a person's knowledge of the truth. It prohibits gossip, the language of hurt, because gossip steals a person's sense of self or their reputation.[5]

The list is long. Hoarding or price-gouging in a time of pandemic or other major crisis is theft. One might say that because the person paid for their seven years' worth of toilet paper, it is not stealing. The Eighth Word calls us to question that casual assumption. When we overconsume, we take from others the basic necessities that make a life of dignity possible. When we resist the boundaries set up to protect the community at large, we steal others' safety and maybe even their lives. When we pit people against each other to acquire scarce resources, that is not just theft, it is theft by violence.

We can do that as individuals, and we can do it as a society. The United States has less than 4 percent of the world's population but we use a third of the world's paper, a quarter of the oil, coal, and aluminum, and 19 percent of the world's copper. Dave Tilford of the Sierra Club tells us that a child born in the United States will create thirteen times as much ecological damage over the course of her lifetime as a child born in Brazil. He goes on to say that the average American will drain as many resources as thirty-five people in India and consume fifty-three times more goods and services than someone in China.[6] When we make our consumer choices, they are more than personal. They have global impacts that give to or take from others for generations.

Much stealing arises from deeply rooted feelings of scarcity. Sometimes that scarcity is real and a legitimate crisis. If a mother is without work and her children are crying from hunger, she may steal a loaf of bread. If a people are long denied justice, they may "take" the streets.

Other times our feelings of scarcity may be exaggerated in our experience. If we believe that there is not enough of something to meet our felt needs, we will grab it however we can. That may mean hoarding toilet paper in a pandemic. It may mean shading the truth to manipulate colleagues to gain an advantageous deal. It may mean stealing hours of our lives searching for the best deal to save two cents on a can of tuna. It may mean stealing the peace in a marriage by being insecure and needy.

Fear itself can be a potent thief. It is a stealthy one, too. Fear is a God-given response designed to help us survive. Over time, however, we can become wired to fear things that pose little threat or to exaggerate former threats and "fear them forward." It is difficult for fear and love to occupy the same thoughts so we can, by nursing our fears unnecessarily, rob ourselves of the experience of God's love, protection, and sustenance.

In the story of the first couple in the garden of Eden, out-of-control desires led to stealing a forbidden fruit, fruit that was set aside for God alone. Fear was the inevitable result of that theft. The fear of being caught led to hiding from what had been the sweetest intimacy with God. Fear of being seen for who they really were kept them hidden from grace that might surely have been offered had they come forward with honesty and remorse. The theft and its response cost them the garden of provision and the direct unmediated relationship with God they had once enjoyed.

In the New Testament, the connection between love and fear is made explicitly. The author of 1 John says, "There is no fear in love, but perfect love casts out fear; for fear has to do with punishment, and whoever fears has not reached perfection in love" (1 John 4:18). The word we translate as "perfect" means full, whole, complete, as intended by God. When fears, either real or exaggerated, take root in the human heart, love is difficult to find and even more difficult to live. The stealing of our assurance and hope by fear is a powerful tool. Used by the unscrupulous to control others, it makes them malleable and therefore easy targets for further life theft.

Stealing from Ourselves

One of the less recognized violations of this Word is the way that we steal from ourselves. We may steal years of life by our diets, our exercise habits, our overindulgences. We may steal our sense of self by choosing to live behind facades and roles we think that those around us desire or require. We may steal our sense of peace and contentment by constantly criticizing our efforts and accomplishments. We may steal our sense of safety and security by developing exaggerated distrust of others or dismissing hope and optimism as unrealistic. We steal our energy by speaking, thinking, and focusing on the negative in ourselves, our families, our churches, and our communities.

We steal our joy and the intimacy of relationships by keeping score and holding grudges. I once had a parishioner come to see me to tell me she was leaving the church. She brought with her a notebook that she had kept for fifteen years in which she had written down every time someone had failed to speak to her, looked past her, not commented on something she had done, and on and on and on. The straw that finally broke her back was that the shoes that I wore on Sunday mornings were shabby! I kid you not. She kept a notebook of grievances for fifteen years! Many of the offenders were long dead. But not to her. In nursing those perceived slights and indignities, she had robbed herself of the joy, humor, grace, and learning of a faith community that was far from perfect but still rich, wonderful, and brimming with love.

Our egos can be powerful, stealthy thieves. Ego, pride, original sin, total depravity, or the false self, however we talk about that wily reality, always takes away from our true selves and the life of blessing for which we are created. Ego's faulty demands never add to our joy, faithfulness, or blessing. This is true even when that false self is telling us that what it is doing and saying is necessary, laudatory, and for our own good. The false self is a thief because it takes us away from the truth of who we are at our core. It replaces that true core self with an endless list of masks and musts that, to chase, can rob us of intimate relationships, creative potential, and ultimately our lives.

Recovering from the Blows

Recovery from theft can be long and hard whether the blow comes from others or ourselves. A trusted friend in a former congregation fell on hard times and stole a hefty sum of money from our women's organization. When the discovery was made, the sense of betrayal was profound. The congregation was divided on how to deal with the theft. People left saying, "If I could be betrayed in this way in the church, I am not safe here." Others left when the church leadership struggled to lovingly hold her accountable: "If the church can't forgive our own, I'm out of here."

She eventually made restitution and moved on in her life, but the damage lingered. There was a scar. What was stolen was more than money. It was the faith community's sense of safety and capacity to trust.

How do we begin to address the wholesale theft of life and property that this Word asks us to reject? The injunction not to steal from others or ourselves that which makes a life of dignity possible, implies embracing its opposite . . . giving that which makes a life of dignity possible. We do not steal; we give. And we do it generously.

Created in the image of God, we look first to God's own generosity to begin to see how we counter our tendency to steal from ourselves and our communities. Throughout the Scriptures we see a God who is lavish with giving. In the beginning, God gives a "garden" of delight filled with beauty, provision, and companionship. When we steal that goodness, God comes up with another plan for a place and a people. All along the way God lavishes forgiveness, prophetic calls to change, wisdom, guidance, and even testing, to help us see ourselves and to make us strong. When we needed more, God gave us God's own self in Jesus, who even gave his life.

God's generosity is an anti-stealing workshop! Because that is who God is, it is also who we are created to be. In Galatians (5:22–23) in his teaching about the fruit of the Spirit, Paul addresses the heartbreaking life-thieves of both legalism and moral laxity by describing in detail what the Spirit gives to those who welcome the gift. Translated as goodness or generosity, Paul uses the Greek word *agathosune*. It means to do good and morally honorable things with complete generosity of spirit, holding nothing back and expecting nothing in return. One way to think about this word is as faith on its feet generously dispensing the values of God. Generosity/goodness is what the

Spirit does in us and through us. It is a thief tamer that can turn our rambunctious, sometimes diabolical, choices to take and demean into the pure energy of love and self-giving.

Generosity/goodness can be intentionally cultivated. To do so may mean unhooking from some of the louder values of our time. The French theologian and philosopher of the mid-twentieth century, Jacques Ellul, believed that the greatest danger in modern life was the idolatry of money, wealth, and security. Like any idol, he claimed, the only way to desecrate it is to use it for a different purpose. To desecrate the idols of greed or possessions, one need simply to give them away. Jesus, of course, prescribed the same action when the rich man came to him asking how to experience the kingdom of God (Mark 10).

If we steal from others by inaction, give action. If we steal from ourselves by meanness, give kindness. If fear leads us to hoard love, money, possessions, then give love, money, and possessions. Open the closed fist and let love flow rather than trying to grasp it for yourself. Grasping what we think we must have will more likely strangle it than bring it to us.

Conclusion

The Eighth Word, no stealing, paints a picture for us of God's intention that all will have enough, exactly what each needs. God's desire is that we live a life of dignity without fear and the grasping hand. To live that way is often countercultural in a world that equates "more" with blessing. To live in this way requires awareness, generosity, healing, and honesty. It is honesty to which we turn in the next chapter.

Spiritual Practice: Actions of Goodness

In the 1980s, I had the opportunity to participate in a short-term mission trip to Central America. While there, we met with theologians who explained the practices of the many house churches that grew up alongside the traditional churches in the area. Several times a week neighbors gathered together in homes or yards for study and prayer. At the end of their time together, each person present made a verbal commitment to one action of goodness to take before they met again.

These brothers and sisters recognized that goodness and generosity are always supported and practiced in community. Sometimes their commitments were small generosities of time or heart. "I will visit my needy neighbor tomorrow and listen to her for thirty minutes. I will not shame her or make her feel worse during that whole time." Sometimes the generosity was more costly. "I will take in the children of my neighbor who has disappeared and share my rice and beans with his widow." Sometimes more costly still, "I will march with the Madres and if I am killed it will be to the Lord." (The Madres were a movement of mothers and allies of those who had been murdered by the oppressive regime.)

To address the ways we steal requires a number of the practices of awareness and justice that we have explored in previous chapters. How have you stolen time, energy, dignity, or resources from yourself or others this week? Could there be ways that you have stolen without knowing? Ask God for insight into those things. Ask if there are ways that you have stolen time from your relationship with God in pursuit of other agendas. Ask God for forgiveness and the strength to live differently.

Examine the last week for times when you have expressed generosity/goodness toward yourself or others. How did you feel? Close your eyes and go back to those situations and replay them. Allow the good feelings to surface again and feel them fully. As you rehearse moments of goodness and generosity, and feel the associated emotions, you begin to retrain your brain toward the positive. Do this often. It is not narcissism when done with gratitude for God's capacity working within you.

Thank God for God's constant generosity to you. Breathe God's goodness deeply into your soul. Then make a commitment to what you will do in order to give to others this week. It may be small. It may be larger. It may be unsettlingly large. Follow where the Spirit leads. Thank God for using you to give and not take from your world.

Questions for Personal and Group Reflection

1. What do you think are the necessary components of a life of dignity? How are those components damaged or stolen?

2. Discuss the Old Testament view of personal property and the claims of God upon it. How does that apply to our lives and cultures? What might a sabbatical or jubilee year look like today?

3. Some have said that not to provide for the needs of others is theft. How do you see this operative today? What societal norms do you think steal from others?

4. How does the misuse of resources steal from the future? How do we give instead?

5. What and in what ways do you see "theft" in our churches?

6. How does generosity act as an antidote to theft? How does love act as an antidote to fear?

CHAPTER 9

⊙⊙

LIVING WITH INTEGRITY

Addressing the Lies That Destroy Us

You shall not bear false witness against your neighbor.
—Exodus 20:16

With Word Nine, God invites us most pointedly to examine our public life, our institutions of justice and our own personal integrity. In the beloved community, our word is our bond.

Appalled by pandemic quarantine weight gain, I walked into Robbie's study, brows knit and patting my hips like that motion could magically shrink them. "Baby," I said. "Do these pants make my butt look big?" My husband looked at me like he was about five years old, had been caught in the cookie jar, and I was his mother asking, "What did you do?" The man knows a perjury trap when he hears one. How could he be both truthful and loving in his response? That is the underlying tension of the Ninth Word.

In its original contexts, this Word was interpreted to focus on the integrity and truthfulness of the legal system.

In Israel's early life, God recognized that it would be impossible for the community to hold together without a bedrock of trust in the system of justice. If one lies in court, justice becomes impossible. Without justice, community becomes impossible.

The emphasis in this Word is on false witness (*eid*) specifically, rather than on false testimony (*eidut*) in general. We are not to testify to the truth of something that we do not actually know from personal experience to be true. We get our legal prohibition against hearsay testimony from this concept. Even if what we testify to is perfectly true, if we do not know that firsthand, it is hearsay, and we are false witnesses. False testimony, on the other hand, is stating that something is true that is not true, or something is not true when it is.

In *Love Carved in Stone: A Fresh Look at the Ten Commandments*, I give a silly example to explain the difference between being a false witness and giving false testimony. Imagine that you get to school and tell the teacher that the dog ate your homework. If you didn't do your homework and you tell your teacher that the dog ate it, you give false testimony. You lie on the stand. If you did your homework, then put it in your backpack to take to school, but it wasn't in your backpack when you reach in to get it, and you remember that you saw your dog acting funny by your backpack, hacking and coughing, and you tell your teacher that your dog ate your homework, but you didn't see your dog actually eat it, you are a false witness. Why? You did not see the act and for all you know your little brother could have done it. In the first case, you lie outright. In the second, you lie by conjecture.

The prohibition against giving false witness, like so much of the moral code at the heart of the Words, is based on a commitment to do everything in one's power to protect the innocent from unjust harm. An unbiased legal system was then, and is now, often the only thing that stands between the innocent and the injustice or defamation that can easily slip in with the testimony of the prejudiced, the unscrupulous, or the exploitative.

In the rules developed to codify this Word into law in Deuteronomy 24:10–25:3 and Exodus 23:1–9, extra attention is given to safeguard the poor in the justice system. Those who have no resources or ability to negotiate the legal systems—widows, orphans, and immigrants—are singled out for special protection. Concern is expressed that their rights not be trampled on by prejudice passed off as truth. The statutes affirm that false witness against the vulnerable is such an important societal sin that, when the poor or vulnerable appeal an unjust verdict, the case is argued directly to God, who serves as their judge. The Bible makes clear that God will not acquit anyone who, through misleading statements and false charges, withholds justice from the poor.

Our biblical ancestors believed that all injustice was rooted in some kind of lie that was accepted by the powerful as fact (i.e. others are lazy, they don't belong here, the land belongs to me, they are thugs and anarchists, and on and on and on). In A Brief Statement of Faith—Presbyterian Church (U.S.A.), the section on sin states, "But we rebel against God; we hide from our Creator. Ignoring God's commandments, we violate the image of God in others and ourselves, *accept lies as truth*, exploit neighbor and nature, and threaten death to the planet entrusted to our care."[1] (Emphasis mine.) Accepting lies as truth always has consequences.

The concern was that lies could be told, believed, and thereby make injustice seem justified. False witness could then give cover for abuse to continue. If this became normal practice, then in extreme cases, injustice could be called necessary and even good. This concern is timeless. Language is powerful and it is a powerful manipulator.

Hannah Arendt, in her 1951 book *The Origins of Totalitarianism*, wrote of Germany in the Third Reich,

> In an ever-changing, incomprehensible world the masses had reached the point where they would at the same time, believe everything and nothing, think everything was possible and nothing was true. . . . The totalitarian leaders based their propaganda on the correct psychological assumption that, under such conditions, one could make people believe the most fantastic statements one day, and trust that if the next day they were given irrefutable proof of their falsehood, they would take refuge in cynicism; instead of deserting the leaders who had lied to them, they would protest that they had known all along that the statement was a lie and would admire the leaders for their superior tactical cleverness.[2]

The biblical writers understood that it was crucial to root falsehoods from the legal system and to expose systemic lies if any semblance of justice was to prevail and innocent life to be protected. They understood that evil always relies on camouflage to spread.

In his beautiful and harrowing memoir, *Just Mercy*, attorney Bryan Stevenson tells his story of graduating from Harvard Law School and coming to Alabama in the hope of fighting for poor people who could not afford representation. In the course of that work, he meets Johnny D. McMillian, an African American man who is on death row after being convicted of the rape and murder of a white woman. Stevenson reviews the case and discovers that it hinges solely on what he believes to be the perjured testimony of another inmate who provided contradictory statements in exchange for a lighter sentence. In this case, by dedicated work and at personal risk, the verdict was overturned, and McMillian was freed. False witness can easily become state-sanctioned murder and not everyone has a Bryan Stevenson. It is the ones who are vulnerable, in particular, that this Word seeks to protect.

A Larger Responsibility

In Exodus 23:1–9, in a section on justice for all, God tells the people that they are not to spread false reports, nor are they to follow the majority into wrongdoing or join hands with a malicious witness. For the beloved community to survive and thrive, the people must stay far from false matters, especially if there is a tendency to become false in order to harm or exploit a neighbor.

Interestingly, this Word is not restricted to behavior in the legal system directly, but also applies to how our words can damage the reputation and livelihood of others. The Hebrew texts for this Word in both the Exodus 20 and Deuteronomy 5 versions of the Words differ slightly. In Deuteronomy the words are *eid shav*. This simply means lying, empty, or vain witness. The concept is similar to what we found in the Third Word when we are cautioned against vain, trivial, or harmful speech against God.

In Exodus, however, the phrase is *eid sheker*. In other instances where this phrase is used in Scripture it is translated as fraudulent or wrongfully injurious. Some early writings translate the Ninth Word as "don't repeat against your neighbor." These teachers saw this Word as forbidding gossip, or any speech that does harm.

Keeping a person's reputation intact was crucial in Israel's social and moral life. To lose one's reputation had both economic and religious ramifications. Because the social order was structured on a shame/honor continuum, the slightest hint of scandal could be dire. The rabbis recognized how difficult it was to recover from a wrongfully injurious testimony or innuendo.

Leonard Felder, a nationally recognized psychotherapist, shares a famous Hasidic story about the dangers of gossip. In this story he tells of a student who has been saying hurtful things about his teacher and spreading untrue gossip. Eventually the student feels guilty about this and goes to the teacher to ask for forgiveness. The teacher suggests, "If you want to make amends for what you've done, I recommend taking several feather pillows, cutting them open, and letting the wind disperse the feathers." The student does as he is told and returns to the teacher, who says calmly to the student, "Now there is one more step. Go out and gather up all the feathers." The student replies, "But how can I do that? It is impossible. The winds have scattered them in every direction." The teacher explains, "Now you are beginning to learn about the power of words. Once you have started to repeat a hurtful rumor and it spreads in all directions, it is very difficult to try to undo all the damage."[3] Avoiding causing injury with our words is a consistent theme in Israel's social and moral code, which forbids, mockery, slander, and self-righteous reproofs.

Medieval Jewish philosopher Maimonides taught that this was so important that if a neighbor needed correction it should always be done gently, in private and only for the other's good. Reproof must be direct and never in public. If we cannot say it to a person's face, we cannot say it at all.[4] In the Bible, shaming a person is akin to killing. Belittling or humiliating others, especially in public, was considered such a grave evil that Jewish moral law questions whether or not a person who does this can ever fully repent.

Our faith ancestors understood that belittling and false speech can be an act of violence that can have lasting consequences not easily repaired. An old Jewish teaching compares the tongue to an arrow. "Why not another weapon, a sword for example?" one rabbi asks. "Because," he is told, "If a man unsheathes his sword to kill his friend, and his friend pleads with him and begs for mercy, the man may be mollified and return the sword to its scabbard. But an arrow, once it is shot, cannot be returned."[5]

Words that wound are forbidden by the Ninth Word, even if they are perfectly true. Wounding words include whisper campaigns to malign a co-worker, innuendo behind someone's back, and even eye rolls when another is speaking. These "words" may be true, but they are designed to lower a person's esteem and to elevate the speaker's.

This kind of false witness can be very tempting. After all, if what we have heard and feel compelled to share is true, we can even convince ourselves that it is our moral duty to share the information. Of course, that may sometimes, although rarely, be the case, if for example, an innocent life is at risk. If that is not the case, however, or if the words are merely slander or malicious falsehoods, no matter how tempting, commentary on this Word over the centuries makes clear that we are to refuse to speak it. The apocryphal book Ecclesiasticus (19:10) gives this warning: "Have you heard something? Let it die with you. Be brave, it will not make you burst!"

Is It Ever OK to Lie?

In general, truth telling is a basic moral obligation in the Scripture. Still, in the Hebrew Scriptures, lying is sometimes more nuanced than we might think. There are a number of exceptions in Scripture to the obligation to truth telling. It is permissible to lie to save a life, to make peace, to avoid injury, to maintain modesty, to protect a person from being taken advantage of, or to keep harmony in a family. Sometimes God instructs a lie. When God instructs the prophet Samuel to anoint David king over Saul, who is suffering from dementia, the prophet is afraid to do it lest Saul hear about it and kill him. God instructs him to lie to Saul and even gives him the words to say to save his life (1 Sam. 16:2).

Even little white lies are sometimes considered moral. The story is told of a debate between the great rabbis Shammai and Hillel about what words are acceptable to say of a bride. Shammai says, "The bride is described as she is." Hillel says, "Every bride is described as graceful and beautiful." The rabbis judging the debate sided with Hillel. A general rule of thumb: for a lie to be justified it must never be told for the benefit of the liar but, rather, always to preserve the life and dignity of one who is more vulnerable.

To swear to something that is untrue is always considered morally wrong and a sin. There are no nuances in that teaching. It is especially heinous because to swear an oath brings God into the lie against God's will. It compounds the evil, violating both this Word and the Third.

Christian theologians have wrestled with these issues for centuries as well. In general, their conclusions are less nuanced, ranging from outlawing all lying under every circumstance, even to save a life (Augustine and Kant), to an understanding that all lying is sin and evil, but it may sometimes be necessary (Aquinas and many of the reformers). Even if necessary, one is culpable for the sin and must atone. The issue at the heart of these positions is that when we make excuses for our lies we can become accustomed to them to such an extent that they become habitual and we can no longer tell the difference between truth and falsehood. To do that corrupts both families and communities.

Our words are a way of loving our neighbors. They are to be genuine and cannot come from a divided heart. The

Talmud teaches that one must not speak one thing with the mouth and another with the heart.[6] In Romans 12:9, Paul makes a similar statement, "Let love be genuine." The word genuine in Greek means not hypocritical, counterfeit, or showy. When we speak words that are loving and kind while grinding our internal teeth and seething, that is also false witness and fails the test of the Ninth Word.

The injunction to truth telling is never an excuse for needless cruelty or verbal sadism. Everything that can be expressed should not, in every case, be expressed. Rehearsing our grievances in our intimate relationships, constantly criticizing a child and forgetting to praise in the name of raising them well, maligning political opponents for no other reason than that it momentarily feels good to take them down a peg, all of those choices wound others and ourselves. In the extreme, demeaning others can lead to dehumanizing the other altogether and result in horrifying abuse that abusers convince themselves is justified. Morality based on the Ninth Word asks us to think before we speak. Is what we are going to say true? Do we know that from personal experience? Is it necessary to speak this truth for the good of another? Is what we have to say fair and upbuilding?

While silence is often the best path if to speak what is really in our hearts would wound another or make us into hypocrites, even silence can be false witness and can do harm. When we are silent in the presence of a racialized joke, or in giving a job reference, or by accepting generalizations of others without question, we, by our silence, attest to what is not true and our discomfort convicts us.

The test of our silence, just as for our speech, is, what are our true intentions in what we say and what we do not say. Will our speech or our silence set in motion dynamics that we cannot control or live with? I remember my father once saying to me, "Genie, don't do anything today that you cannot tell the truth about tomorrow." The truth matters. It matters in court and it matters in our personal and societal relationships.

What Is Truth?

But what happens to us as God's community when we can no longer figure out what truth is? When truth is about spin, when even observable facts are debated and debased, when truth appears to have versions, what do we do?

In the fall of 2019, I watched some of the public hearings of the impeachment of President Trump. What became clear very quickly was that the divisions in our country are not about different strategies for solving problems or setting priorities. Rather, they are rooted in belief in two diametrically opposed "truths." Everyone is so certain, and they are certain of things that cannot both be true. It was wrong. It wasn't wrong. Which is it?

A part of the problem is that, in our time, lying is commonplace and even normalized to keep or to gain power. Truth becomes secondary to power, or just to saving face. When that is the case we lose our ability, or willingness, to trust witnesses who testify under oath if they do not support the outcome our preconceived worldview requires. At that point, truth ceases to exist as a meaningful and determinative reality at all. Even a cursory reading of history tells us that any ideological or fear-based system will eventually distort reality and resist transformation.

There are indeed ideologies that are false in and at their core. Their bedrock itself is a lie—a lie that is adept at disguising itself as truth to the unsuspecting. White supremacy is such an ideology. It and its tenets, both subtle and profane, are a lie. There is no science behind it. It was made up in order to give cover to behaviors that exploit, to gain power or to shore up feelings of inferiority and victimization.

The problem with these kinds of systems' lies is that when we try to dismantle the systems, some of the lies are so subtle, especially if they have no part in our conscious experience, that we do not address them. We have accepted them. Even talking about the system and its evils is mediated through the lens of the lies we do not or do not want to see.

The National Book Award winner Ta-Nehisi Coates, in his book *Between the World and Me*, makes this point clearly:

> But all our phrasing—race relations, racial chasm, racial justice, racial profiling, white privilege, even white supremacy—serves to obscure that racism is a visceral experience, that it dislodges brains, blocks airways, rips muscle, extracts organs, cracks bones, breaks teeth. . . . You must always remember that the sociology, the history, the economics, the graphs, the charts, the regressions all land with great violence upon the body.[7]

Systems of oppression rest on lies that are underground, unstated, or sugarcoated. They are based on unspoken or veiled words that, over time, or quickly and brutally, dehumanize another for someone's benefit. The early interpreters of the Ten Words understood that to spread lies that humiliate is just like killing a person. When we magnify this offense and apply it to groups or peoples, it far too easily leads to genocide.

The situation in which truth seems illusory, manipulatable, or dependent on personal preference is exactly what God tried to protect us from in the Ninth Word. The truth does not have versions. It certainly has interpretations, but not versions.

Our current struggles with the truth are not new. In presiding over Jesus' trial, Pontius Pilate, the Roman official

charged with determining guilt, asks, "What is truth?"
(John 18:38). That question and all of its ramifications has
come down to us through the centuries as our own. When
we listen to the news, what is truth? When our child comes
home and tells us where she has been, what is truth? When
we are asked to give a deposition and our memory is fuzzy,
what is truth? When we speak of another, what is truth?
When we set our priorities, what is truth? When we examine our heart, what is truth?

To speak the truth in a context in which those with
power in our lives are deeply invested in the lies, is dangerous business. Retaliation against whistle blowers, the
arrest of peaceful protestors, firing and threatening orga-
nizers for fair working conditions are a few examples of
the cost that speaking truth, especially to power, can have.

The Cost of Deceit

The early church fathers and mothers understood deceit to
be a major block to spiritual living. Sometimes called van-
ity, or vainglory, deceit is a cardinal vice. It is so dangerous
because, over time, when we lie enough, especially about
ourselves, we cease to be consciously lying. We become the
lie and it becomes us. Satan is called the father of lies in the
Gospel of John (8:44) for that reason. He not only lies, it
has become his identity. He no longer tells lies. He is a liar.
When we as humans allow our lies to control and define
us, we have entered into bondage of our own free will. Lies
require a great deal of maintenance. The first casualty in a
life of lies is our freedom. Second is our sense of self.

Sometimes, we are tempted to be false witnesses to ourselves about ourselves. Perhaps we would never dream of
lying in court or to our spouses, but we know how to lie to
ourselves.

The phone rang at a very inconvenient time. It was in the spring of 1971. I was sixteen and busy in my room making flowers out of crepe paper while the glue dried on my newest collage. I was feeling very self-righteous. I had taken a stand. That year was the year of total integration in the schools in my little south Alabama town.

A casualty of adult fear in those days was the prom. It was too terrifying a thought that young people of different races might dance together, so it was nixed. At one point, heeding the outraged cries of their children, some parents got together and decided that they would have separate proms. One for black kids, and one for white kids. I would have none of it. I remember the feeling of righteous power I had as I ran up and down the halls telling anything that breathed that, as for me, I wasn't going.

But that night, Tim, a senior, called and invited me to go. Suddenly, all I could see in my mind's eye was him in a powder blue tuxedo to match his eyes and me in peach taffeta shaking away to some terrible band with the scent of Old Spice and gardenias in the heavy air. Torn between my warring desires, would I be my own false witness? Would I find a way to make it seem OK?

There are ways of living that are honest and ways that are utterly dishonest. The way we live is our truth, no matter what we say. Sometimes living out our truth is costly to us and to others. Did Tim and I go to that prom? No. We rode around all evening in his Camaro listening to music on his old eight-track tape player. He missed his senior prom because he honored what was important to me at that time in my life. It was a small victory tinged with self-righteousness for me. It was a bigger victory of integrity for him. Loving-kindness and personal sacrifice were his witness. That has stuck with me all these years.

The Ninth Word invites us to be true to our deepest selves and our values. Saint Anthony of the Desert, an early

Christian mystic, went into the wilderness in order to live a more authentic life than he felt that he could surrounded by the world's flurry and temptation. He taught that in order to love God one must learn to love one's own soul, essence, self. He believed that to love God we had to also love God's image in ourselves, just as God made us. To do that, we have to find a way to see and speak truth to ourselves.

Often, in opposition to welcoming our true selves, we exaggerate both our failings and our successes. Both of those things leave us bereft of the sweet truth of who we really are, an amalgamation of the glorious and the profane, inescapably human and inescapably precious. Unraveling the lies we tell ourselves about ourselves is spiritual work. If we begin to accept the lies as truth we will soon lose sight of who we truly are.

The lies we tell ourselves are sometimes put in place early in life. We develop them to navigate our environments and sometimes to survive them. In chapter 6, I told the story of my friend whose mother punished and shamed him early in his life for getting into her lilies of the valley. Later that wound and many others festered in him to the point that he once told me that he was such a liar that he would lie when it would be just as easy to tell the truth. I suggested that he might need to talk to a trusted therapist to help him sort through all of this. He said that he could not do that. There was a toxic waste dump of pain inside him. He believed that if he looked at it he would drown in it. Truth can take us to places of pain before healing comes. True healing, finding the true self and experiencing God's delight, cannot, however, happen in an atmosphere of lies.

It is never too late to do the work of finding and appreciating our true selves. It can be painful to see the truth, especially when, as we look back, we begin to see the harm we have done to ourselves and others along the way. It has been said that hell is truth learned too late. Still, our faith tells us that there is no such thing as too late when we are embraced by the love of God. The mystics of the faith have a name for this sacred sadness that comes from seeing our failures of integrity. It is called compunction and is itself a healing grace. Without it, we may *look* good, but we will not *be* good.

Becoming a Faithful Witness

To be a faithful witness to ourselves we have to attend carefully to the words we speak to ourselves. Are they true? Are they necessary? Are they fair? Only when we take the log out of our own eye and begin the journey of seeing ourselves, our values, and organizing our lives consistently around those truths, can we be trusted to see clearly the failings of others and find loving ways to help individuals and communities address them.

In the Old Testament, integrity is spoken of as righteousness, *tsedaqah*. It means to do the good thing, to do the God thing in every circumstance. It means to stand blameless and true before God, oneself, and one's community. The opposite of righteousness is to live with a divided heart. It is to will contradictory things and to find oneself whipped around by the hurricane winds of following different paths. To live with integrity is to follow the path God sets.

The New Testament writers use words like faithfulness and purity of heart to talk about the way of life into which the Ninth Word invites us. Purity of heart simply means to do one thing with all of one's effort and dedication. To be pure of heart is to know who one is and to live consistently from that knowing. We cannot know who we are, and who we are before God, and be willfully cruel or lying with our mouths. It will not be long before our words become actions and we become strangers even to ourselves.

The antidote to lying or cruel words is obviously true and kind words. To refuse false witness is to actively choose to speak in ways that bring life and esteem to those who hear our words. To be a faithful witness is to find a way to speak truth in love and always and only for the good of the hearer.

Pat Hoban-Moore, chief administrative officer for the U.S. Department of Housing and Urban Development, tells a story about growing up in Chicago in a large Roman Catholic family. One of twelve children, she was age six when her mother was stricken with terminal cancer. Pat remembers near the end of her mother's life that family friends took each of the children downtown to buy new outfits for their mother's funeral. Pat bought a beautiful little dress complete with matching shoes and socks. She said that even at age six, when she tried those nice things on in the department store, she knew she looked beautiful. Her mother's friend complimented her on her choice and said, "Oh Pat, when your mother sees you in this dress, she will feel so much better."

Pat arrived home just as the priest was leaving the house after offering last rites. When Pat saw this she ran upstairs and put on all her new finery. She went into her mother's room to show her. "Oh Pat," her mom said weakly. "You look so lovely."

"But Mama," the little girl said, "but Mama, do you feel better?"

Her mother, with all the strength she had in her body, called her child close to her and said, "Oh yes. Yes, I feel so much better. And Pat, I want you all your life to do what you can to help other people feel better."[8] While some might have found those words of Pat's mother to be fraught and hard to live up to, for Pat they provided great love and gave her the mission statement of her life. In those final words, Pat's mother thanked her child and blessed her with purpose.

Words that bless can heal even the deepest wounds over time. While harsh words linger, kindness works its magic as well. Words spoken with integrity out of love and not self-interest can be direct encounters with divine love and set in motion healing that unfolds over years. Truth heals those who honestly want it and who are willing to turn from the lies to lives of integrity and purity of heart.

In a time when truth is difficult to ferret out and not always valued when it is, perhaps we can only begin to heal as individuals and as a society from the deep wounds inflicted on us by violating the Ninth Word by making a commitment to revival of personal integrity. We can only begin with ourselves.

Conclusion

The Rev. Dr. Martin Luther King Jr. once said, "I refuse to accept the view that mankind [*sic*] is so tragically bound to the starless midnight of racism and war that the bright daybreak of peace and brotherhood [*sic*] can never become a reality. . . . I believe that unarmed truth and unconditional love will have the final word."[9]

In giving us the Ninth Word, God reminds us that in the beloved community unarmed truth and unconditional love will indeed have the last word in our lives. They must, or our community will not stand for long.

Spiritual Practice: Journal Keeping

Joan of Arc is said to have prayed the same prayer each day: "If I am in your truth God, keep me there. If I am not, God, put me there."

In John 14:6, Jesus tells his friends that he himself is the way, the truth, and the life. Invite Jesus to help you to see the ways that deception and false witness may be damaging your life, family, and community.

Try keeping a journal for forty-eight hours. In it, write down every time that you give voice to an unkind, gossipy, or false word about yourself or someone else. Note any unwarranted or unkind criticism. Make a note of how you felt and what you think led you to say what you said. Guard your tongue and ask yourself when you feel an untruth or unkindness rising up whether what you are saying is true, necessary, and fair. Ask yourself who is helped and who is harmed by your words.

Recall a circumstance in which you deceived yourself or violated your own truth. Settle your heart and remind yourself that you are safely held by God as you do this reflection. Bring to mind the time, place, situation, and persons involved. Pray softly the simple prayer "love and truth" for several minutes. Then ask Jesus to show you what urged you to deceive yourself. How did you feel? Is there a pattern of self-deception in certain areas of your life? Ask Jesus for the grace to be honest and to see yourself in God's love. Ask for strength to see yourself clearly in all your messy humanity. Don't worry if your memory is vague or faulty. God will work with whatever you bring.

Close your reflection time by praying again, "love and truth" and allow the awareness of God's presence to grow in you.

Questions for Personal and Group Reflection

1. How do you understand the difference between being a false witness and giving false testimony? Can you think of examples?

2. Former Senator Daniel Patrick Moynihan famously said, "Everyone is entitled to [their] own opinion, but not to [their] own facts."[10] Some today have suggested that we live in a "post fact" era. In what way do you observe this? How does the Ninth Word address this idea?
3. Can you identify a time when words were spoken that set in motion consequences that could not be turned around?
4. What do you think are the central qualities of integrity and pureness of heart?
5. How do you understand the concept of the true self versus the false self?
6. Discuss in what circumstances, if any, lies might be moral?
7. In what circumstances do you find it most challenging to tell the truth?

CHAPTER 10

ENOUGH

Addressing Desires That Substitute for Life

You shall not covet your neighbor's house; you shall not covet your neighbor's wife, or male or female slave, or ox, or donkey, or anything that belongs to your neighbor.

—Exodus 20:17

During the early months of pandemic isolation, Robbie and I moved into my ancestral home. It is the home my father was born in, died in, and I lived in for the first eighteen years of my life. Both the old house and I are showing our age. The first week that we sheltered there we woke to discover that raccoons had gotten into the house and helped themselves to anything they wanted in the kitchen. Robbie and I slept through the whole thing. As we were cleaning up the mess and trying, without success, to find a local trapper, a violent storm blew through and we lost power. At the moment the power went out, the airbrushed image of the beautiful beach house in the Hamptons that features in the movie *Something's Gotta Give* came into my mind and I caught myself thinking, "If I just lived there everything would be perfect." Was I coveting a neighbor's house—even if that neighbor was fictional?

The Tenth Word brings us full circle in the picture of what God desires for our lives and the life of the beloved community. It is perhaps the most startling Word of them all. It is the only one of the Ten that seems to command the reining in of an emotion—and a pretty common one at that.

Coveting is not the same thing as envy. Envy is that feeling of displeasure or discomfort we have on hearing of the good fortune of others or when we see what they have that we might want to have as well. Covetousness is something deeper. It is the desire for something that is so deep it easily becomes predatory. It is not just the desire for something. It is the desire to supplant something or someone.

The problem with covetousness is not just that we want something. There is nothing wrong with wanting in and of itself. Desire is essential to life. If we don't desire to eat, we starve. If we don't desire to be loved, we don't risk loving. The issue is what we want those things to do for us. Desiring becomes coveting when we come to think that something we don't have can fix our lives, and therefore we must have it, are entitled to have it, and cannot be happy or content without it.

Years ago, after we had moved to a new city, I was excited that my then husband and I were going to welcome guests for the weekend. I didn't have sheets for the new guest bedroom, so I headed to the department store to buy some. On my way to the linens, I passed through housewares. On a display stand, surrounded by glitter and pictures of smiling families, was a machine whose sole purpose was to puree tomatoes. I was mesmerized and I wanted it. I thought to myself, "If I have this machine, I will puree tomatoes and make homemade spaghetti sauce." The unspoken part of that inner dialogue was, "And then my husband will be happy with me." That moves desiring into coveting.

This Word is related to the other nine and, if left unexamined, can lead us to violate them all. Covetousness can lead us to believe that something other than God can salve our wounds, free us, manage our emotions, and become our little gods (Words One and Two). It can lead us to misuse God's name, "O Lord, let me win the lottery!" (Word Three). It can rule us to the point that we never stop and rest, to see God's provision or work for God's justice (Word Four). It can blind us to seeing what and who really brings us to life (Word Five). It can lead us, metaphorically or even literally, to kill anyone who gets in the way of our getting what we want (Word Six). It can lead us to cheapen our relationships (Word Seven). It can lead us to steal (Word Eight). And it can lead us to lie about it (Word Nine).

More Than Simple Desire

Again, covetousness is not simple desire. Covetousness is predatory desire. The Hebrew text helps us understand this. In the Exodus version of the Ten Words, the word is *chemdah*. *Chemdah* refers to the overwhelming desire to own or possess something that is physically lovely, close at hand, and irresistible. This term is always used in the present tense and results in concrete actions. When caught up in *chemdah*, a person is oblivious to consequences.

Chemdah is the kind of desire that we see in the story of King David and Bathsheba (2 Sam. 11). One day David sees the beautiful, married Bathsheba taking a bath on her rooftop as was the custom. He is overwhelmed by her beauty, acts on his desire, and disaster ensues, including the murder of her husband, the death of the child conceived by their union, and estrangement of his sons who learn from his behavior.

A clue to understanding how *chemðah* takes hold is found in the first verse of the story. "In the spring of the year, the time when kings go out to battle, David sent Joab with his officers and all Israel with him." We know immediately that something is amiss in the story because David does not go with his troops. It is the time when kings go out, but this king stays home. Something is wrong in David. He is ripe for falling. This is how *chemðah* works. Something is amiss inside me. I see something that I think will make me feel better. I want it. I take it. I care nothing for the consequences. I have to have it. *Chemðah* is sudden, explosive, and has long-term consequences, not just for the coveter but for all involved.

In Deuteronomy's list of the Words, the phrase is different. Here the writer uses the word *ta'avah*. *Ta'avah* describes a subtler and more interior experience of desiring. It refers to a deep yearning, a pining for something. The longed-for thing or person may or may not be beautiful. It may or may not be physically present. It can be the yearning for something, or simply *the yearning for something else*. It is the kind of yearning that takes root in the heart and grows over time, eventually taking up room inside a person that was meant for other things. *Ta'avah* can take over one's life and even lead to despising it. While *chemðah* is sudden and irresistible, *ta'avah* creeps in and metastasizes. *Ta'avah* can erupt quickly and focus on something in particular, but usually it has been restlessly at work for some time.

The story of the downfall of King Ahab and his wife Jezebel (1 Kgs. 21) gives a picture of the disastrous effects of this kind of covetousness. Ahab, while not the worst king that Israel ever endured, was not a significant force for moral good either. He professed to follow the God of Israel. He was married to the strong-willed Jezebel, who was a follower of Baal, the chief god of the Canaanite and Phoenician religions. Ahab is castigated in the Bible for trying to make a place for religious pluralism in Israel.

One day Ahab decides that he wants a vineyard that adjoins the palace and belongs to a faithful Israelite named Naboth. Ahab sends emissaries to Naboth to offer to buy the property. The land was considered a sacred inheritance and it would have been a great shame for Naboth to consider selling it. He refuses.

This so upsets the king that he takes to his bed for three days, turning his face to the wall and refusing to get up, eat, or rule the country. He is consumed by his thwarted desire, to the point that he despises his whole life. Restless and unmoored by his desire, he is undone by it. Jezebel, frustrated with her husband's weakness, tells him to get up and get at it. She will take care of everything. She hatches a plot to have Naboth killed by trickery after telling him he is being honored at a community celebration. She hires mercenaries to kill him and secures the vineyard. This so outraged God that it nearly destroyed Ahab and cost Jezebel her life. This is covetousness run amok.

The Basic Lie

Not all longing is covetousness, however. Sometimes our longings come from deep within the soul. We long for justice to rain down like waters. We long for love to come to us and ease our achy hearts. Sometimes, we long for concrete things that we need, food to feed our families, medicine to cure our illnesses, health care that we can afford, or a safe place to live and a good education for our children. We long for a chance in this world and for others to have the same chance. We long for an authentic life that we somehow know exists but seems beyond our grasp.

The real problem comes when deep and authentic longing for the good devolves into the basic lie that everybody else has it easier or their lives are more together, prosperous, or exciting than our own. When we choose "I am down, and you are up" as a life position, it minimizes our ability to see and celebrate the life we have with all of its gifts and urgencies. We distort our own struggles, imagining that others are somehow lighter or easier to bear.

The Tenth Word recognizes that when we compare we despair. Our house will never be as perfect as we imagine our neighbor's house. Our marriage never as fulfilling. Our celebrations never as spectacular. Our jobs never as brimming with satisfaction and opportunity. When our hearts are somehow hollowed out by thinking that the grass is always greener, covetousness rules and we, like Ahab, can see nothing left but what we do not have. Our authentic inner longings become lost as invitations and guides to our deeper selves and callings. All we want is to duck the invitation and find an elusive equilibrium that stops our discomfort.

There is also a subtle difference between covetousness and jealousy in the Bible. Jealousy is not envy, which simply feels bad and wants something someone else has. Jealousy is marked by a competitive spirit, wanting to have an advantage over another. It is advancing one's rights to the exclusion of another. The word is often used of God's zeal for us, or of the zeal of the faithful to advance the cause of God. With covetousness it is not so much competition for advantage, as it is the drive to *replace* the other person in order to acquire what that one has for its medicinal or anesthetic value. In the story of Ahab and Naboth, Naboth was utterly irrelevant to Ahab. It was not about him at all. It was about getting what Ahab wanted, not somehow besting Naboth. Covetousness makes others expendable to our desires. Jealousy, while often deeply problematic, can also be a motivator. Covetousness is always a thief and a liar. It has no positive application.

Covetousness can metastasize in communities and societies. The biblical writers and the early commentators saw the primary danger of this word to be rampant greed, especially greed on the part of the powerful. In the Hebrew scriptures, covetousness is generally seen as a problem of the wealthy. There are frequent warnings against the appropriation of land or property for the most powerful from the least powerful. This is especially fraught when, as with Naboth and Ahab, the advantage is linked to political power.

The dynamic of the powerful taking what they want when they want it is not unknown to history, both biblical and secular. Israel takes the land, at God's behest they believe, from the native inhabitants and one invading power after another takes it from them. Colonialists take land from native peoples. Settlers "buy" Manhattan for beads. Hitler moves into Poland. Russia into Crimea. The powerful taking what they desire, while concocting elaborate justifications for their actions, is not just the stuff of ancient times.

The covetousness of the powerful was even evidenced during the pandemic. While millions of Americans were losing their livelihoods, and with them their health insurance, and were being thrown from their apartments and homes, the richest in the United States saw their wealth soar. Amazon's CEO Jeff Bezos added $34.6 billion to his wealth in the first three months of shutdown. Facebook's Mark Zuckerberg picked up $25 billion.[1] Granted, both Amazon and Facebook have filled a real need in this time. But still, what is really enough? And upon whose labor is this wealth accumulated? At whose expense? As Thomas Mann put it in his commentary *Deuteronomy*, "Enough is what most of us would be glad to have if we didn't see others with more."[2]

What Is Enough?

It is easy to see how an obsession with wanting things that others have and we don't can make life a misery. We all can recognize that. We can even recognize that we already have most of what we need, if not more than we need. We even recognize that what we need and what we want are two different things. The passion behind our needs and wants comes from different sources. Our needs come from the basic quests for safety, survival, and creativity. Our wants often come from buried wounds. Covetousness preys on wants and not needs. It looks for a wound and festers there.

It is perfectly proper to desire what we need, especially if we are in a situation of the lack of justice. That is a very good thing because it gets us to stand up for ourselves and the change that is needed. Covetousness is something different. Covetousness is rooted not in lacking something we need. It is rooted in the sense that we ourselves are somehow lacking and that something outside of ourselves can fill that hole and address that fear.

When we do not feel like we are enough, it is very easy to substitute things (possessions, a promotion, accolades, a new relationship) for deeper things. That is the danger that God is trying to help us avoid in this Word. God does not want us to listen to the story that our possessions tell us and fail to hear the real story that God is telling in and through us.

The invitation to reject predatory desire is God's way of removing from us those things that block us from living authentically and powerfully as we are now. Covetousness pushes everything into the future. "I will be happy when . . ." and we reject, despise, or simply fail to notice the now, with all of its small and winsome graces.

It is even possible for nostalgia for what we once had to become predatory in our thoughts and emotions to such a degree that our lives become painful and our grief toxic. After my retirement last summer, I struggled for months. I mourned for my church and my life as a pastor to the point that I was miserable. I cried every day. My home is just across the street from the rectory of the Episcopal priest in our town. Every Sunday I watched her get in her car and head to her church and I was filled with not just wanting my old life back but I coveted my neighbor's life. I was like Ahab looking at that vineyard. I didn't have and couldn't have what I wanted, and it nearly consumed me. It consumed me to the point that I totally idealized the last thirty-five years of ministry on the one hand and was dissatisfied with what I had accomplished on the other. This went on for months. It is perfectly possible to covet what was and what wasn't as much as what is and what isn't.

An initial glimmer of sanity finally got through to me when I remembered an example that a colleague once shared at a retreat. Trying to illustrate the power of Christ to heal our wounds, she went to the baptismal font for an experiment. She took two Styrofoam cups, a ball point pen and a big pitcher of water. She filled one cup with water and told us that we were like the cup, filled with God's love and grace. As she talked about the wounds and failures of life, she took the pen and punched holes in the cup. First a trickle, then a flood as the grace seemed to drain away with each hurt, or moral failing. When the cup was empty, she placed the holey cup inside the second cup. She asked us to imagine that the second cup was Jesus patching up and forgiving everything. As she did this she poured water into the cup and never stopped pouring until the cups overflowed into the font.

When I was in my despair, that image came to mind and I saw myself as a cup full of holes punched by my out-of-hand desire for my life to be different. I realized that God wanted nothing more than to fill my life with grace and wonder, but I was draining it all away by wishing for something else. For me in that moment, the cup that healed was not only Jesus, but gratitude. Gratitude for what had been, certainly, but even more, gratitude for what currently was. It was a new moment of becoming.

It is also possible to lapse into predatory desire that hampers daily living by desiring an emotional state so strongly that we mold life, ethics, and energy around finding the key to it. If we covet romantic love, we may look in all the wrong places and to all the wrong people to find it. If we covet a feeling of victory, we may become obsessed with a sports team, candidate, or day at the track. If we covet peace, we may become violent in the quest for it. If we covet spiritual highs, we may become dilletantes flitting from practice to practice and never learning the gifts of the desert.

To covet an emotional state is not the same as a healthy desire to find love, emotional security, or well-being. That desire is what helps us not give up on ourselves and our practices. However, descending into predatory desire for them becomes slavery that leaves us laboring for a harsh master who never has our best interests at heart. It is in this state that desires become obsessions and obsessions become compulsions. Our lives are lost to the chase and we move through them in a kind of catatonia, never seeing what is, who we are, or who God is, for the sugar plums that dance in our heads.

The Invitation to Authenticity

In urging us to reject predatory desiring, God is simultaneously calling us to lives of authenticity. Rejecting covetousness addresses the compulsions of our lives and makes space for them to be healed. The intimacy, belonging, and purpose that we truly crave cannot be met by others or by our dramatic refusal to be ourselves in order to please or lure them. Brené Brown puts it this way, "True belonging doesn't require you to change who you are; it requires you to be who you are."[3]

The ever-fresh surprise is that God loves us as, how, and where we are. Our job is to wake up to that love and our true identity. God begins the Words by telling us who God is, that God loves us and longs to free us from every hurtful bondage. God ends the Words by asking us to love God by loving ourselves and releasing the tendency to use things and people as drugs to numb us to the lives we are living now.

An Invitation to Release

The invitation to release predatory desires asks us to make space for something different. In a sense, the Tenth Word asks us to practice one of the great paradoxes of the faith, that we die to live. Only when we are empty can we be filled. The Ten Words in general, and the Tenth Word in specific, are a manual for teaching us how to die to the false self with all of its compulsions in order to rise to the self we were always created to be. The Tenth Word helps us let go of the harmful things that drive us and cause us emotional pain. It reminds us that what we cling to, whether that is a dream of acquiring what we have decided is the good life, or the dream of being a different person altogether, will inevitably become our enemy. It will blind us to who God really is and only serve to reinforce our own illusions that keep us at arm's length from others and ourselves. Our predatory desires lie to us about what will actually feed and nourish us. We cannot repair our wounds with stuff. When we try to do that, we ourselves become the prey.

In his book *Who Dies?*, Stephen Levine says, "If you made a list of everything you own, everything you think of as you, everything that you prefer, that list would be the distance between you and the living truth."[4]

Jesus recognized this in his encounter with the rich man (Mark 10:17–22). In this story, a rich man comes to Jesus feeling restless to his core. He has abided by all of the rules of the Law down to the letter and still he does not feel that he is living in the kingdom of God. Something is off. Something is missing. Jesus listens to his story, and with breathtaking poignancy, the text tells us that Jesus looked at him and loved him, then told him that he only lacked one thing. He should sell his possessions, give the proceeds to the poor, and come, empty-handed to follow Jesus. Shocked and grieving, the rich man turns away. He was willing to do anything but let go of his possessions. He could not imagine life without them and so he turned from life itself to keep them. A wise spiritual director once said to me along the same lines, "If you have something you cannot release, you do not own it. It owns you."

In the Tenth Word, God asks us to refuse a life of greed and the restless feeling of never having enough, especially when that greed is turned upon our neighbors and is exercised at their expense. God does not say, don't desire a house *like* your neighbor's or a spouse *like* your neighbor's. God says do not desire *that* house or *that* spouse because the line between what we desire and what we are willing to do to acquire it is thin and easily crossed. King David taught us that.

In the fourth chapter of Ephesians, the author tries to help the struggling church recognize that life in Christ is completely different from the life they see lived in the surrounding culture. All around, the daily life of others seems ruled by greed and predatory desires. He warns that that rule leads to hardness of heart and the inability to recognize the truth. Instead, he urges them to submit to a spiritual revolution of their minds, to see the old ways, the false self, for what it is, and to see new life in Christ, our true self, as it is. We are to put on the true self like a new suit of clothes, a suit that fits perfectly and reflects the truth because it is the truth. In other words, our stuff is not who we are. We are created in the image of God, beloved, and no acquisition will improve on that reality.

Antidotes to Covetousness

The tendency to substitute things, people, or the fleeting euphoria of acquiring, for authentic living cannot, in my experience, be tamed by sheer dint of will. There are only two things powerful enough to do that, both gifts of God that can be developed but require constant renewing grace to live out. The first is a depth of humility or gentleness that allows us to look honestly at who we are and stay in the present moment with peace.

In the Beatitudes (Matt. 5:1–12), Jesus quite startlingly says, "Blessed are the meek." The word meek or gentle is a concept in Greek that defies easy translation. The Greek word, *praus*, refers to one's inner attitude toward God in which, from the core of who we are, we accept God's dealings with us, God's very self, as good. Therefore, we live our lives honestly, gratefully, and without disputing or resisting. Rather than a word that connotes weakness or sad resignation, *praus* connotes power and centered confidence. This state, which Paul says in Galatians 5 is fruit of the Spirit, is the opposite of self-aggrandizement or predatory self-interest. *Praus* is a calmness of spirit that is neither elated nor deflated because it knows itself so well that it is no longer even occupied with the self and its grasping ego. This Spirit-given meekness recognizes that as our true selves, tucked into the heart of God, we have everything and therefore need nothing.

The other powerful covetousness antidote is gratitude. Gratitude is the key factor to a life of joy and bounty. When we can discipline ourselves to see the grace and goodness of life, even when it is difficult, then we become transformed and usable creatures. Several years ago, I was undergoing painful and frightening tests at Stanford Medical Center. As I waited for the next round one day, I wandered into the gift shop in the Cancer Center and saw for sale a simple bracelet with the word *gratitude* on it. I bought it and as soon as I put it on, I felt a shift in my heart. Suddenly a day that was filled with discomfort on so many levels became an opportunity for me to "put on" thanks and praise for the wonders of a God-graced life.

When God is our number one, as the First Word declares, then love is our constant companion. When that is the reality we claim, then gratitude can become the lens through which we view the world. This change of lenses dramatically affects every aspect of life. We find the clutching fist of acquiring and neediness release our hearts and we become more interested and inspired by giving than getting. Grateful hearts cannot contain themselves. They are forever leaking love and generosity into every corner of the world. We then make decisions from hearts filled with gratitude and not scarcity or fear. Gratitude is born from the recognition that God is not limited and therefore we don't need to hoard or worry or entertain restless longings nearly as much as we do. When gratitude is born, covetousness shrinks, and we know deeply that our needs have been met.

A number of years ago when I was pastor of an urban church in Birmingham, Alabama, I had the opportunity to work with a man who spent his life aiding the most down-and-out in the city, particularly those who were addicts living on the streets and alleyways downtown. He did his work with such simplicity and power largely because he himself had been there. He knew the life, the passions, the excuses, the hurdles that had to be leapt in the lives of those who had lost everything.

One hot July day, we were sitting on the front steps of the church having a glass of cold water and he told me his story. He told me about the knife fight in the back alley that had left him bleeding and holding in his guts with his hands until someone went for help. He told me that right then he decided that his life had to change. He told me about the people who walked by and averted their eyes from the nearly 300-pound bleeding Black man in the street. He told me he hadn't used since that day and he told me about the enormous gratitude he felt toward Jesus for his rescue.

What really struck me was something that he said at the end of our conversation. He said that he thought that people who had always been in the church, who had lived pretty good, pretty moral lives, who had never messed up all that much, never been in real trouble, have no idea what grace is and don't have the same sense of gratitude that he and the ones he worked with had.

"For them, the 'pretty good at being pretty good' ones," he said, "it's not so much about what God has done for them as what they still want God to do for them." Something more. Something else.

When we live with predatory desires consuming our lives and communities, we live in fear, fear of scarcity, fear of not having enough, and fear of never quite being enough. Our focus is on what we lack, rather than what we have been given. Ahab lived in a palace but took to his bed over a vineyard he couldn't with integrity acquire.

We cannot overcome the tendency to covetousness without knowing the grace of God deeply and daily. Otherwise we will just substitute one deceit for a better-disguised one.

God's way of healing always gives more than it ever asks us to relinquish. We don't live to die with the most toys. We die to live with the most love. When we say yes to this calling, over time, we begin to develop the capacity to listen only to the voices that lead to life and not those that cannot be trusted.

When I was serving as a pastor in Colorado, our youth group and sponsors went on a short mission trip one weekend to a tiny town in southern Colorado called San Pablo. San Pablo was a desperately poor, high-spirited town located in a sweeping green expanse of valley rimmed with 14,000-foot snow-capped mountains. One of the projects for the weekend was to help paint the house of one of the church members who was physically impaired.

The small, ranch-style house sat on a rise on acreage that was in large part used to raise sheep. When the young people and I arrived at the ranch, we headed straight to the fence that separated the sheep from the side yard. We called and whistled and did everything but turn back flips to entice the sheep to the fence so that we could scratch their black noses. They would have none of it. They didn't even lift their heads. Shortly, a neighbor came out to us with a paper plate piled high with carrot curls. "They love these," she said, heading to the shed to look for a ladder.

So we tried again. No luck. Finally, the kids just threw the carrots curls and turned to go about their work. I lingered for a moment by the fence. When I turned to head to the house, I remember thinking that it was no wonder there were so many references to sheep in Scripture. They may not be all that smart, but they know which voices to listen to, they know who will be there when winter comes, and they know who is fleeting and will never see them through.

The fleeting desires that can so consume us will never see us through the harsh times in life either. God knows in giving this Word that only as we turn from those allurements will we be able to turn to, to have room for, that which will really see us through.

Word Ten is about the sacred journey to yourself. It is about letting go of the clutching fist of things and expectations. It is about waking up to who you really are in the present moment as God's deeply loved and celebrated child. The Words start with love and end with love. Words two through nine show us what living in love looks like in human life and community. Word Ten asks us to wash away the allurements that masquerade as success and sink into the beauty of the moment, expecting only the goodness that God will provide.

Conclusion

The great eighteenth century Rabbi Zusya was renowned for his wisdom and yet struggled his entire life to be somehow more and better than he was. The story is told that when he was on his death bed his students gathered around him and asked him for a final word. He told them, "When I arrive at the heavenly tribunal, I shall not be asked why I was not Moses, why I was not Jacob, why I was not more like the fathers. When I arrive at the heavenly tribunal, I shall only be asked why I was not Zusya."

There is more to the Tenth Word than a cautionary tale about predatory desires and where they can lead. Tucked into the heart of this Word is God's desire that we live the lives we have been given to the fullest, in the moment, where we are, how we are. God begins the Words with self-revelation and asks for our embrace and commitment to God alone. God ends the Words with asking us to embrace our own lives and make a commitment to our true selves, releasing the grasping hand with which we reach out for covering or to lay hold of the anesthetic du jour.

With Word Ten, God closes this provocative declaration of love and well-being with the call to live with authenticity and presence in the lives we live. Faithfulness does not mean that we must be perfect. It consists of simply knowing who we are and living that to the best of our ability in love of God, love of neighbor and cherishing of the self.

Spiritual Practice: Gratitude Again

The great Christian mystic Meister Eckhart once said that if the only prayer we ever pray is "Thank you!," it is enough.

Gratitude is the heart's response to the reality that our gifts always outweigh our burdens. It, like love, is a choice. It is independent of circumstances because it is rooted in the unchangeable reality of God, not in what is temporarily going on in our lives. To live in gratitude requires spiritual grace, to be sure. It is, however, a practice that can be cultivated.

One of the hindrances to practicing gratitude is that we think that we must look for the big things. The truth is that gratitude practice is most effective and enduring when we recognize the grace of small things. In her book on mercy, *Hallelujah Anyway*, Anne Lamott opens with a poem by Naomi Shihab Nye called "Famous."[5] In the poem she talks about the perspective changes that I believe the Tenth Word calls us to examine. She celebrates her desire not to be famous for achievements. Rather she declares that she wants to be famous like a buttonhole is famous, simply because she never forgot what she could do.

To teach the practice of gratitude, a few years ago I ordered several large sacks of marbles online. When they arrived, I put a large bowl of them and a clear mason jar by the baptismal font and invited worshipers either before, after, or as they came forward for Communion, to take a marble representing something specific for which they were grateful and put it into the mason jar. That way we gathered our gratitude into a visual display. When the jar was full, they did not want to stop the practice. So we ordered more marbles and more jars and kept the practice up throughout the summer. Our blessings were so many we finally ran out of room!

Perhaps you might want to try this practice at home. Try getting two jars and place them where you will see them often. In one put a marble or, if you can't get marbles, just a colorful note of gratitude for a specific blessing or kindness you have experienced. Do this every time you notice the jar, even, or especially, if you are not feeling very grateful, are worried, or just out of sorts. Do the same thing with the other jar, only in this jar place a marble or note thanking God for an aspect of yourself for which you are grateful. It can be a kindness you offered to someone, or a moment when you held back a harsh word, or a feeling of hopefulness that broke through. It can also be for just who you are, warts and all. Especially warts. When we thank God for all of who God has made us, for the grace so lavishly given, there will be no room for wanting more and no desire for someone else's life!

Questions for Personal and Group Reflection

1. How do you understand the difference between *chemdah* and *ta'avah*? Can you think of examples?
2. Where do you think the line falls between a normal healthy desire for something and covetousness?
3. What do you see as the most important consequences of covetousness in communities? How do you see it operating?

4. What are your culture's values about acquiring and having? What about giving?
5. How do you think various media feed the tendency to covet?
6. When you think about turning from covetousness as a turn toward the sacred nature of the present moment and your own true self, what questions or insights does that raise? What emotions?

CONCLUSION

Be patient toward all that is unsolved in your heart and try to love the questions themselves. . . . Do not now seek answers, which cannot be given to you because you would be unable to live them. And the point is, to live everything. Live the questions now.

— Rainer Maria Rilke[1]

Perhaps if you have read this far, you have more questions than answers arising in your soul. Hurray! When viewed in the ways that I have suggested, the Ten Words do indeed initiate a great paradigm shift. The way we see God, ourselves, and our communities can feel topsy-turvy. Like the dove sent forth from the ark to fly over the watery chaos, we may want to go back because we can't find a place to rest our foot. Remember to be gentle with yourself and stay open to how God is working in your life through the invitations of the Words. The new paradigm that God is always calling us into is so much finer than the small windows we have on the world. The new you that God continually calls into being is finer than anything that you must set aside to lay claim to it.

Some people, when they approach the Words in a deeper way, find that they feel overwhelmed with guilt.

People who thought that they had never violated any of them find that they do so routinely. Sin is a reality. It is not possible to avoid completely in this life as hard as we try. That is why we are so grateful for God's start over grace in Jesus Christ. Remember that forgiveness is always available. It is more than a mere transaction that balances a cosmic scale. It is also a revelation, an appearing. It is a process where we peel back layer upon layer of illusions and self-deceptions. It is honest bearing of the soul that starts the true healing process.

The Ten Words are words of love that frame our lives, give them shape and safety. Returning to the symbol of the mandorla (the almond-shaped frame formed at the intersection of two circles, symbolizing the intersection of divinity and humanity) that we discussed in the introduction, we can think of the Words as a divine embrace, filled with passion, warmth, protective instinct, and parental desire. When we dwell within the mandorla of the Words, we dwell within the heart of God. God becomes our dwelling place and Christ is both our host and our guest. In this dwelling place our oneness with God is both spiritual and ethical.

In the Words we see not merely a list of requirements. We also see the very nature of God and God's values on display. The Words are God's self-disclosure.

Word One: God is loving, self-giving, and freeing.
Word Two: God is the only one who can save us and desires that we cling only to Godself.
Word Three: God is one who desires deep intimacy, shares power with us and asks that that power not be misused.
Word Four: God is one who invites rest, who provides totally, and who delivers justice.

Word Five: God is one who brings us to life and asks us to give precedence to those God uses to bring us to life.

Word Six: God is the one who holds death and life and who values all life.

Word Seven: God is our *ezer kenegdo*, the one in whose presence we are safe to become all that God has dreamed.

Word Eight: God is the one who never takes from us and who desires a life of dignity for all.

Word Nine: God is Truth and desires truth for us.

Word Ten: God is enough for us and we are enough for God.

With each disclosure, God reaches out to heal a wound in the human heart and the human family.

With Word One, God addresses the fundamental loneliness to which the human heart is prone.

With Word Two, God addresses the confusion of searching for wholeness anywhere but with God.

Word Three addresses the pain we experience when we trivialize God and try to use God like a puppet on a string.

Word Four addresses the life-sapping busyness that substitutes for life and the enslavements of our need to be in control all the time.

Word Five addresses wounds of families and the need to open ourselves to all that brings us life.

Word Six addresses the kill energy that can take over our lives with hate and violence.

The Seventh Word addresses the wound of flimsy commitments and broken relationships.

The Eighth Word addresses the hurt of taking the easy way out at the expense of others' dignity.

The Ninth Word addresses the wound at the heart
of a culture, or a life, that can no longer tell the
difference between truth and lies.
Word Ten addresses the restlessness of not knowing
who we are in the moment and the pain of thinking
that things can make us happy.

For many of us, it took Jesus in order to see what it
means to live according to God's values in human life. The
blessing is that God only tells us to be what God already
is (1 John 4:8). The Words are for the purpose of nurturing love, intimacy, and soul. We are never "ourselves"
if these values are not the frame that both contains and
illumines us. Likewise, we are never fully in Christ until
we release ourselves into who we really are. The Words,
while certainly law in the sense of covenant agreement,
are a checklist for authenticity and integrity as well. They
are a touchstone to which we return again and again to
get our bearings in a world often ruled by other rules. In
approaching the Words, we find both personal and com-
munal healing. It may not always feel like it if our view of
God is punitive and we think that the world around us is
coming apart at the seams, but it is always the case.

As you dive deeply into the healing power of the Words,
I leave you with the benediction that I almost always use
in my congregations. It is adapted from an old monastic
benediction.

May God bless you with discomfort, at easy answers,
half-truths and superficial relationships so that you
will live deeply and from the heart.
May God bless you with anger at injustice, oppression,
and the exploitation of people so that you will work
for justice, freedom, and peace.

May God bless you with tears to shed for those that
   mourn so that you will turn their mourning into joy.
And may God bless you with just enough foolishness
   to believe that you can make a difference in this old
   world, so that you will do those things that others
   say cannot be done.

NOTES

Chapter 1: Greeting the God of Love

1. Rachel S. Mikva, ed., *Broken Tablets: Restoring the Ten Commandments and Ourselves* (Nashville: Jewish Lights, 2001).

Chapter 2: Looking for a God That Sparkles

1. Thomas Merton quoted in Richard Rohr, *Breathing under Water* (Cincinnati, OH: St. Anthony Messenger Press, 2011), 102.

2. This phrase was popularized by Anais Nin, who attributed it to Rabbi Shmuel ben Nachmani in the Talmud. Christopher L. Heuertz, *The Enneagram of Belonging* (Grand Rapids, MI: Zondervan, 2020), 39.

3. Heuertz, *The Enneagram*, 16.

Chapter 3: Language That Lifts

1. For more of Emoto's fascinating work, see Masaru Emoto, *The Hidden Messages in Water* (New York: Atria, 2005); *Water Crystal Healing* (New York: Atria, 2006).

2. Name changed.

3. Leonard Felder, *The Ten Challenges: Spiritual Lessons from the Ten Commandments for Creating Meaning, Growth, and Richness Every Day of Your Life* (New York: Harmony Books, 1997), 76.

4. Felder, *Ten Challenges*, 71.

Chapter 4: Just Stop

1. Abraham Joshua Heschel, *The Sabbath: Its Meaning for Modern Man* (New York: Farrar, Straus and Young, 1951), 13–24.

2. Preaching Pastors' Seminar, May 5–7, 2015, Zephyr Point Presbyterian Conference Center, Zephyr Cove, Nevada.

3. "Arthur Ashe Quotes," BrainyQuote.com, www.brainyquote.com/quotes/arthur_ashe_371527.

Chapter 5: It Takes a "Crash"

1. Rising from his experience with the Truth and Reconciliation Committee in post-Apartheid South Africa, Archbishop Desmond Tutu and his daughter, the Rev. Mpho Tutu, provide insight into true forgiveness and practices for healing through forgiveness in their book *The Book of Forgiving: The Fourfold Path for Healing Ourselves and Our World*, ed. Douglas Abrams (New York: Harper Collins, 2014). I cannot recommend this book too highly if you are ready to go more deeply into forgiving parents, others, or even a broken culture.

Chapter 6: Murder Most Foul

1. Terence E. Fretheim, *Exodus*, Interpretation: A Bible Commentary for Teaching and Preaching (Louisville, KY: Westminster John Knox, 1991), 233.

2. Alexa Smith, "Rattle Fatigue," The Holy Land Christian Ecumenical Foundation, August 27, 2001, https://hcef.org/453-rattle-fatigue/.

3. For a wonderful treatment of the subjects of rage, shame, and grace, I recommend Lewis B. Smedes, *Shame and Grace: Healing the Shame We Don't Deserve* (New York: HarperCollins, 1993).

4. For an interesting treatment of individualism and its results, see Robin DiAngelo, *White Fragility: Why It's So Hard for White People to Talk about Racism* (Boston: Beacon Press, 2018), 9.

5. Trudy Ring, "Anti-LGBTQ+ Alabama Mayor Resigns After Denouncing Black Lives Matter," Advocate.com, July 3, 2020, https://www.advocate.com/politics/2020/7/03/anti-lgbtq-alabama-mayor-resigns-after-denouncing-black-lives-matter.

6. Francis Brown, S. R. Driver, and Charles A. Briggs, *A Hebrew and English Lexicon of the Old Testament* (London: Oxford Press, 1959), cited in Leonard Felder, *The Ten Challenges: Spiritual Lessons from the Ten Commandments for Creating Meaning, Growth, and Richness Every Day of Your Life* (New York: Harmony Books, 1997), 130.

7. Felder, *Ten Challenges*, 131.

8. John Calvin, *Sermons on the Ten Commandments*, ed. and trans. Benjamin W. Farley (Eugene, OR: Wipf & Stock, 2019).

Chapter 7: Worthy Companions

1. *The Anchor Bible Commentary*, vol. 1 (New York: Doubleday, 1992), 82.

2. See Eugenia Anne Gamble, *Love Carved in Stone: A Fresh Look at the Ten Commandments*, 2019–2020 PW/*Horizons* Bible Study of Presbyterian Women PC(USA), p. 72, for more information. The midrash are interpretations of the Hebrew Scriptures written down by rabbis in the first, second, and third centuries CE that supplied answers to contemporary questions.

3. Rainer Maria Rilke, *Letters to a Young Poet*, trans. M.D. Herter Norton, rev. ed. (New York: Norton, 1954).

4. Ellen Amy Ryles, *With Scars on My Soul: A Story of Release and Redemption*, (Maitland, FL: Xulon Press, 2014).

Chapter 8: To Catch a Thief

1. Leonard Felder, *The Ten Challenges: Spiritual Lessons from the Ten Commandments for Creating Meaning, Growth, and Richness Every Day of Your Life* (New York: Harmony Books, 1997), 180.

2. Yiddish is the language that evolved in the European Jewish diaspora during the Middle Ages. It combines elements of Hebrew, German, and Slavic languages and is used by some to this day.

3. Patrick D. Miller, *The Ten Commandments*, Interpretation: Resources for the Use of Scripture in the Church (Louisville, KY: Westminster John Knox, 2009), 324.

4. Robin DiAngelo, *White Fragility: Why it's So Hard for White People to Talk about Racism* (Boston: Beacon Press, 2018), 48–50.

5. Rachel S. Mikva, Lawrence Kushner, et al., *Broken Tablets: Restoring the Ten Commandments and Ourselves*, (Nashville: Jewish Lights, 2001), 103.

6. Doug Moss, "Dear EarthTalk," *Blue Ridge Outdoors*, Sept. 12, 2014, https://www.blueridgeoutdoors.com/go-outside/united-states -consumption/.

Chapter 9: Living with Integrity

1. *Glory to God: The Presbyterian Hymnal*, (Louisville, KY: Westminster John Knox, 2013), 37.

2. Eugenia Gamble, *Love Carved in Stone: A Fresh Look at the Ten Commandments* (Louisville, KY: Presbyterian Women, 2019), 95.

3. Leonard Felder, *The Ten Challenges: Spiritual Lessons from the Ten Commandments for Creating Meaning, Growth, and Richness Every Day of Your Life* (New York: Harmony Books, 1997), 185.

4. For a broader discussion of this teaching, see Rachel S. Mikva, ed., *Broken Tablets: Restoring the Ten Commandments and Ourselves* (Nashville: Jewish Lights, 2001), 113.

5. Joseph Telushkin, *Words That Hurt, Words That Heal: How to Choose Words Wisely and Well* (1996; New York: HarperCollins e-books, 2010).

6. Mikva, *Broken Tablets*, 117.

7. Robin DiAngelo, *White Fragility: Why it's So Hard for White People to Talk about Racism* (Boston: Beacon Press, 2018), 89.

8. Pat Hoban-Moore (speech, Leadership Birmingham, Alabama, class graduation ceremony, May 29, 1998).

9. Martin Luther King Jr., "Martin Luther King Jr.—Acceptance Speech," NobelPrize.org, www.nobelprize.org/prizes/peace/1964/king /26142-martin-luther-king-jr-acceptance-speech-1964/.

10. Daniel P. Moynihan, *Daniel Patrick Moynihan: A Portrait in Letters of an American Visionary*, ed. Steven Weisman (New York: Public Affairs, 2010), 2.

Chapter 10: Enough

1. Robert Frank, "American billionaires got $434 billion richer during the pandemic," CNBC, May 21, 2020, https://www.cnbc.com

/2020/05/21/american-billionaires-got-434-billion-richer-during-the
-pandemic.html.

2. Thomas W. Mann, *Deuteronomy*, Westminster Bible Companion
(Louisville, KY: Westminster John Knox, 1995), 89.

3. Christopher L. Heuertz, *The Enneagram of Belonging* (Grand Rapids, MI: Zondervan, 2020), 58.

4. Stephen Levine, *Who Dies? An Investigation of Conscious Living and
Conscious Dying* (New York, NY: Doubleday, 1982), 182.

5. Anne Lamott, *Hallelujah Anyway: Rediscovering Mercy* (New York:
Riverhead Books, 2017), xi.

Conclusion

1. Rainer Maria Rilke, *Letters to a Young Poet*, trans. M.D. Herter
Norton, rev. ed. (New York: W. W. Norton, 1954), 27.

Printed in the USA
CPSIA information can be obtained
at www.ICGtesting.com
CBHW072212050924
14184CB00028B/351